I0751025

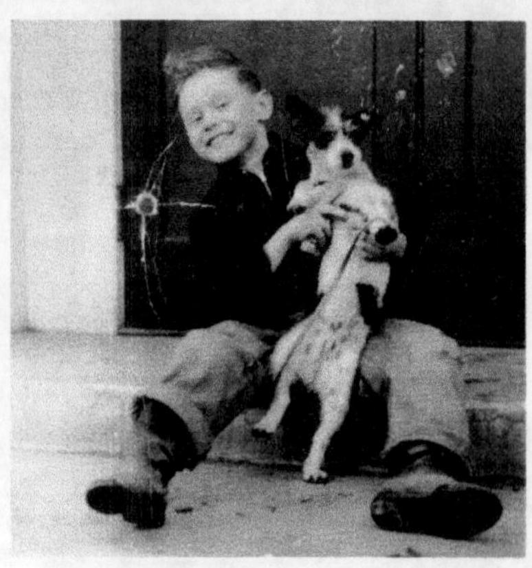

About the Author

Lloyd Patrick Baker, born 1929, is an artist who's elegiac words and striking photography, composed over decades, still ring with prophetic verity today. He regards this opus as a reflective journal that takes on surrealistic tones as he combines his interests and experiences as a child of the high desert and the Great Depression. Growing up in the Klamath basin as the son of a uranium miner, Lloyd became politically aware at a young age after observing the treatment of Japanese Americans in the internment camp in Tule Lake, CA. As a child he studied taxidermy, ballistics and was one the first in Oregon to practice falconry. He served as a photographer in Germany during the Cold War and upon his return home continued his study of art the Portland Art Museum School. Lloyd has a BA and MFA from Indiana University and was awarded a Fulbright grant to study ceramics in Finland. A passionate activist since his youth, he fought the dumping of over 25K barrels of 2,4-D and Agent Orange ingredients in Eastern Oregon, and has been a vocal witness against the destructive nature of man and war.

Lloyd's poetry is enriched by his love of Eastern Oregon and a life-long engagement with languages, etymology, geology, ornithology, archaeology and history. He combines popular expressions with his own unique form of line, rhythms, and word forms. His poetic voice is unique, somber, challenging and engaging for those of serious mindset about today's events and the questionable future we face.

Ephemera

Poetry and Photography by Lloyd Patrick Baker

Chapters

Ephemera
Poetry and Photography

Published in the United States by Wasabi Cat Publishing,
Seattle, WA 2016
www.wasabicat.com
ISBN: 978-0-9963433-0-5
Library of Congress Control Number: 2016935635

Dedicated to Marian Angele, my amanuensis.

Special thanks to Chelsea Leach for her invaluable contribution to making this book possible by finding so many lost and damaged pages of poems and transcribing them from rough handwritten script into readable format.

Preface

I tried to say goodbye to the world yet I remain
to take charge of myself and this long poem, and its
welling up again, the green wave, my continuous song to Oregon,
coming on strong and white-capped, sung to you
who know its dense mountain cover and cryptic geologies,
you who celebrate the world primordial, our origins,
our grey stones, our wide margins.

- Lloyd Patrick Baker

Goddammit!
Where is she when I need her?
Psyche! I might abandon her
to Odin's arctic North,
to his raven messengers
Huginn and Muninn!

This is the endlessness of blackness,
pay umbrage to somber deity
churning the bed where magma was sleeping
tools are made ready, ready to make everything
a large serpent lies dormant, coiled in my mind
fight or flight—it is muscular and oiled
its eyes pupils like slits
deep within saurian bone.

The dawn, in its preciousness.
Believe in its importance,
even during oppression
when the dancers fall exhausted
and birds swelter within shelter of desert leaves,
with their beaks half-open
waiting out the heat.

Stars are tears in more than trillions,
and greater is the weight in funeral sorrow
than in joy of birth.
The place, the time—it will happen.
I can tell you neither climate, nor season,
but know that it will be and we shall all be there.

But for yesterday, for Jester Death,
I peopled my eternity not with faux ritual
or shallow excuse.
I smelled the mountain lily,
and tasted genius at its root.

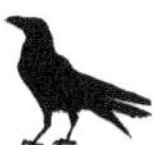

-fragment from the lost Medea play by Lloyd Patrick Baker

That very evening Artemis whispered from eternity
that I should make free an ode
from gray powder and cindered stone,
from ash that was once a sacred forest.
Here and now with my two hands
at the apostrophe of apocalypse,
In this parenthesis of catastrophe
wherein may be counted among the dead
my awakened man-hairs gray as Athena's.
Blackened stelae with unreadable inscriptions to gods once known,
swarthy Christian crosses yet smoking among the litter
of tonsures and hoods, the quick dust devils,
where stood dithyrambic maniacs shrieking at the future for the past.

Powder, rust, death, the gray-eyed rocks that have seen
everything under these suffocated stars.
where this forest has given up all of its poetry.
There, I found it—under a blue fragment,
a crazed egg shell. The ode I've set free is a prayer.

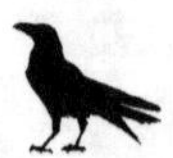

With the poem's bass voice shuddering,
echoing the tolling bronze,
do you hear now how the poem is within us
with its own voice which may go unheeded
as the ravens nudge one another
on the sea cliffs, crying out for carrion?
Spoken on the lips of the poem
is the mouth of the muse compelling and oracular
and layered deep within the
poet's transient life.

Amygdaloidal Basalt

Book 1

Childhood & Nature

A Letter Home

A long day after
the bewildering rain,
with the visage of this place,
as usual, dark and unsteady,
the blear of radio tells us
of the not too distant calamity.
I have discouraged the alibi,
which I'm certain
you'll be glad to hear.

I summon you under dire wind
where louts shoot eagles
for pastime.
Under grinding dust
advancing armor,
we must be quick to learn a way
past the unburied dread.

Field sparrows call in truest colors
only to disappear in time and territory
to reappear as tears
across the thunderstorm.

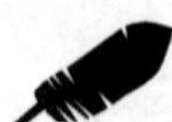

Slick Leaf, Mahogany

A whole hillside of slick leaf and lacquered mahogany in full sun,
and a hill cast in watchful shadows as I gaze across the water.
All the birds have molted and stags have shed their antlers, a time of
heat and rumors and browsing sounds from the observing shade.
I shouted thrice like Pan and set tremors through the waving firs and
junipers.
Black trout hugged their rocks, their white slits breathing in the
darkness.
That careful watching figure, standing behind the curled leaves,
a mule-deer.
The hornless buck flaring my scent, stamped twice, vanished, spied me
again from the backtracked path
on my way in the waving wilderness.
Buck musk and other odors over pollen colored water,
drifting pitch, the yellow eddies, curled catkins, overhung.
A time of heat and lizards bobbing as I passed the cut bank, rubbing
lichens, tapping rocks
waking the spirit.
The sky rising wind, steady on red tail sails, the armored feet,
the summer bees, their bodies impaled on the shrike's thorn.

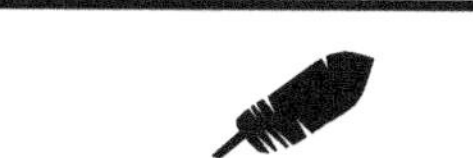

Age-fallen,
this tree could be that hollow canoe
we pushed past the ripple stone,
current turned,
our last chance floated past.
Only a fallen tree,
rough timber
enough to frame and shake a house
with stairs to climb,
limbs enough
to warm a winter.

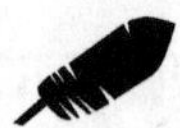

All colors in evening iridescence burn
in the cloud of violet flies.
And at the end of September that resembled summer,
we witnessed it written that something very interesting
was seen, although somewhat erased by nights with
failed moons.
Strange spots developed in our eyes
and after waves without sound or motion,
the feverish ocean too soon
stretched out its soft grays to the dead.

As light plunged,
and the shadow fell,
that usual anxiety at day's end
when standing at the terminator,
did you hear me cry out to clutch the lateness?

Did you witness then the spread of mauve
stabbing the sky in an instant blood red?
And was that roar heard over the trees,
night hawks searching for ghosts?

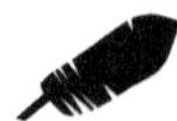

Enough of this. Take me back to the stream.
Help me cast off this annual skin, like the snakes.
The swelling aches.
The stigma reappears; gives the omen momentum.
And with the shadows quickness the boulders are molten.
My eyes were green, back at the stream, where first I washed
my spots.

Assassin beetles have kissed
the corners of my night smile.
Light again is born in blood.
The deity mumbles
with a swollen mouth
and man takes no heed.

The sky is muted
in infamy and scandalous fog,
reddening,
this dirt besmirched in anger.

White riving boron at the mordant borders,
cerements on the blinding shores
where the evening primrose showed,
with sifting sastrugi its petals blow.
Its seeds scatter uselessly at my feet.

Wind stings my face.
All birds fall silent,
waiting for the lake's last arsenic
to fill my sight with disgust.

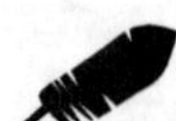

Autumn is a rattling month. The wind.
Hunger is a sallow face. The starving sit.
At once shrunken and distended,
bones and swollen paunches,
bellies bloated parchment;
when harvest fails.
Fields yield their scarcity to the mowers.
and visitors take note.
Yellow clouds from the fallow ground,
follow the striving gale,
ground rutting and exhausted in the winds.
Man, the laborer gathers,
on haunches, migrant,
ditched with voracious locusts,
sheltered with dearth
and dried stalks.

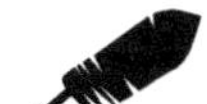

—In a homestead plot in Sherwood my family lies together,
the stones nearly touch
in the warm summer drone of flies and birds.
Aunt Margret complained, "How the weeds have grown.
I can't read the names."
I told her, "Let them grow; we are weeds."
My humor, like my father's,
"Hell, let them grow," he said.

I loved her grey eyes, tender, grave—so tired.
Three horses stood at the iron fence.
"It grieves me to see horses bleed, how they suffer," she said.
It was the time of year warbles work layered hide;
horse blood rains, birds pester wounds, fester. Bots fly.

I spoke of ancient art, of red running down ceramic legs and
sides of Sung ware, of Chinese scrolls,
the horses seeping crimson paint, blooded by flies.

That dank swift shearing Willamette song,
warblers' and finchs' insistent songs
Margret spoke so softly in the stratum between their arias,
"Cruelty is not a proper subject for art."

—Stunned, seldom do I argue among stones.

My grandmother washed her Irish hair in rainwater
caught in the barrel at the corner eave.
At the corner eave, rainwater caught for her,
the leave taking, the secret work being done,
she washed her Irish hair in rainwater.
My grandmother, in rainwater,
washed her Irish hair.

—Black in the continuity, my existence is a hole;
life caves in upon—from behind, following me through.
—Moments detonate—I am left without meaning; do I know
what's going on! I ask myself was that what I meant to do, to hear, to
    see, to say?
—I have reared no children unless he be this strange one
within, my own unsuccessful child.
My summer blond hair only once.
Existence feels spherical, curved in
rings and layers: ring within rings, in layers—a day lily which is first an
    onion.
—Not even the gods see its purpose, nor would they care;
for since my birth I am done for. I thought of that
when it took two hands to lift a glass of milk.
Would they ever grow to uncle size—and when they did, would I die?

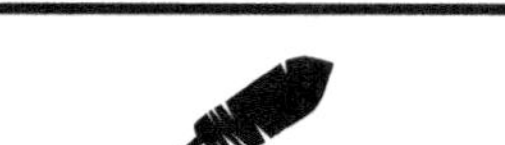

Autumn light oblique on evening trees casts long soft
shadows engulfing sage, smooth stones,
rooting through bottoms and washes
to awake the nocturnal from unseen burrows and webs.

Scarlet lichens turn magenta and mauve
from the dark that pours down from the rift
and wraps us together in a basalt blanket.

Now the effable stargaze falls
at the terminators nearly lost catch moment
when the failed sunset's blood
and the grave Artemisia's fallen purples
with its gray green leaves are lost to shadow.

Diurnal focus dissolves to night; stars begin.
With soft galactic eye, Andromeda watches
across the talus slant, the angle of repose.

Under vast, sidereal shift
The seasons tire, tilt and disappear.
The vipers emerge through the smudge of night.
Time has fallen, horizons cohered,
with the dark eternal crush loaded with stars.

Behold this hand-held stone.
Behold again the granite hands at the verges,
my hands among them, at the edges
where the active massif shows
its most brilliant fractures.
Here age after age
the faulted face reflected
the eagle's echoes.

But this mantle has vastly changed:
Tremors foretell gray ash fall.
Speak to the derelict, adrift as dust
or to the stone ground
finer than gravel, coarser than sand,
that, in little time, wears rocks round
such as these smoothly whitened crania
of a half-buried army,
or these ejecta worn to size,
no larger than fists,
piled now in a new mound
no longer than an old man.

Black porphyry
black my cat
amber eyes wink on the darkness,
comfortably she moves closer
as I move restlessly,
stirs an easy place on my arm.
Onyx nails holding looser.
The long teeth barely show;
below the vermilion mummy tongue
slips out, in speed with thought.
From spines' graceful descending line,
falls the tail,
charms the curl around her feet.

Ragged flocks are settling,
falling with the barometer
as evening ears tilt toward
the dark's familiar geese
flying in from Canada,
thrashing heavily at the landings,
as she purrs her eyes asleep,
purrs my eyes asleep.

As a lone goose drops
across the crescent moon,
I think of an ibis a-whirr
somewhere far
over the warm Egyptian river.

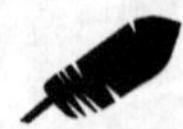

Blossoms stay till aspens quake within their own white bark
in the yellow blaze the freeze shall extinguish
and winter's quail fly.

Grebes call across the water
with that moment of avocets flying
as far as midnight
with lonesome song.

Death haunts the living trees:
long lines of veins search
with root tips amid sleeping forms
feeling between ancestral sediments.

Bones have no eyes—cannot cry.
Bones the flash floods drift.
Bones frail in alluvial grind,
ground in a water which annihilates forever
—all ending in the pool together.

Have you heard these contrails with radios whisper,
watching downward with sinister eyes?
Trees speak—bones dry—quail fly,
as leaves fall away.
and somewhere, in the high Cascades,
it snows.

Black Hole

Children of dreams and night
    it was greedy god who chewed the first
        black hole
            in heaven
    deep beyond the primal dissonance.
In the ongoing and chiming dust
        beyond Magellanic clouds
            where he first swilled
        the think cosmic cream
and thickened it to flowing magma
    increasing and reducing:
        entering the angry inevitability
    rushing faster within itself through
            yawning mouth
where ends all light in the brightest gravity.
            The flow ends
    collapses as the ultimate solid with
all orbits crushed in the ending squirm:
        electrons ceasing, protons vanishing
            atoms touching
at the very limit of singularity become the
        totality of matter
harder than diamonds
    rounder than space
        heavier than time

and remain in extremis as the invisible grin
    until devouring Chaos again
        gives back his children.

Crouched in forest corners,
profound surrender,
smoke low at the horizon,
living among rocks,
rupestrine.

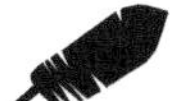

Blue sky, flawless precious sky,
look up as we lie;
even during the sun's day
we are exposed to the cosmos.
Only the frail blue holds us in,
shields us from the frozen blackness.

At night we lie before the stars,
spinning loose in the dreams of astonishing orbits.
And now I know we've swung away,
too far, beyond our own apogees.
We stand apart in our lonesome apostasy,
but we are a part of everything
in our beginning dreams and death.

Can we live heedless of the stars, in dull security,
never gazing upward?
Hurrying in from treacherous city paths
never looking upward—give us this day our daily bread—
secure in danger lying comatose before the cathode tube
grazing contentedly in shopping centers
tranquilized in the trivia soporific
lulled in suburban dailiness.

Four drought years and pines die;
the frantic seeds cast wide and the lake dries,
heaves up its grey ribs off shore;
from the mud that holds our settled bones,
rocks emerge, ash and cones;
waters recede from cemented shores;
and we're all struck dumb
by the awesome centuries
that grip our histories.
In that distant year of the last tide,
horst and graben assumed their oblique angle.
The years trail as fingers in our common blood.
Short were the shadows from the quick sun.
—Beautiful that long, low note your lips blew
through the long-emptied shell.

I fear that never again will the bullfrogs fill the silence with fable,
but tonight all night long the frogs cry out for god.
I fear the morning might be made of death
and the clouds clotted and without movement
antique grey.
I know crabgrass will inhabit the cracked asphalt.
I know a weary dog will follow the day,
that an ominous shadow follows me
cuts my trail and backtracks
sometimes lying in wait beside a boulder, a dark pool.
A shadow calls across the black river, barks from the ravine
the shadow I cast, the shadow that dogs my heels as usual.

Piety is that migration of evening grosbeaks bringing
to the juniper gold and ceremony.
The day's poetry is the lark filled with berries and phonemes.
Berries are the religion of birds.

As noon ignites the day, horizons burn
the rocks crack to show their calcium trails of frozen yearning.
The earth rolls on its escapement, ticking as days tick,
like seconds before the sun's great dial.
There is something most erotic in the way this wind is panting.
A wind from far away breathes across our lives from all directions
uncovers us bit by bit under the wide sky's blue and white gauze.

I cannot find your face in this place aslant in memory
where pages fall open to a space with white walls
and unfinished pictures and blue tile
and all the doors ajar with angled light and that sunset
which even today remains unbelievable.

The gravid cloud filled with memory empties
as shades one by one assume their final positions
in the aggregate.

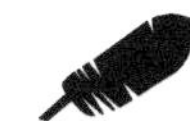

In dream's ontology
my being swells with night birds and songs
the words unformed, untold, unsung.
I dream the egg and within the yoke
slowly winding on polar threads
in amniotic syrup
twisting life's anchored threads
at the world-womb,
a lone figure in a landscape eternal
where the bulldozer has never left a track.

From autumn rocks shots ring out
to murder the ear.
Wounded ducks fall to the ice
and slide vermilion streaks
to murder the eye.
The stag dressed in Manzanita
is discovered with the shout
that murders the word.
Do you think my behavior strange
when I complain of the pale
miasmas rising with portents
from rotting tule peat
when I taste danger in the
ominous air in shearing
fronts of startling weather
when land is expectant,
bristling, erect with hoar frost
waiting for skeleton winter?
Remember this:
I too am disturbed by murder.

At the cliffs I have posted sentries
to guard the moonrise
over vast dominions
of grey gravel and white bones
all alert to the river's sexual odor
to the smoke that feeds upon the roots
in the fossil forest
and to dream-walkers talking,
telling too much,
and to every movement
granting no forgiveness,
all mindful of the windless moonrise
and a mottled skyscape.

No night longer than these staring roses.
No light stronger than that black star
in the dinosaur's eye.
Everything's eaten!
Greedily we're sent reeling
toward our final
bloated sunset.

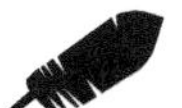

I was abandoned in the night, for I was not born
with a silver spoon, but the moon in my mouth.

The earth always escaped me, the meaning,
the riddles of the geese, the bones—
    frail sockets watching eternity—
the old gyration, the endless possibility, the plenitude,
with this goddess undressed in unimaginable infinitude.

A long snake of a sentence that hunts for hidden access
through which occluded edges create the vignette,
confronted by the unapproachable, I expect the irrational,
as the breeze becomes bereaved,
as these geese crossing the sun burn my eyes
as the distance erases their passionate language.
Geese with magenta moons in the nights of my fingernails,
with the holes in perfection burning my heart.

And You, resurrected, come yawning from the grey dream
where color and speech were muted,
might rise with the angry sun to find the wind
risen in waves to gale force,
a tide seething the junipers, undermining,
excavating our ancient race buried
with their tongues extended
that they might consume the moon.

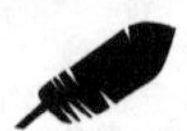

In this wide void of the future,
clearly I see our future as if it were
not void but an alarming text,
clearly writ and deliberate
with scant erasures.
I shall think of the rainforest
and the macaws which deserve
a future just as much as I.
How I wish my voice could
take on the sound of the syrinx.

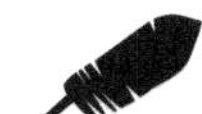

The beaches, my natal beaches, boneshed on dunes
closer to the apsis region farthest from farther point
from wooded plateau in sepia aquarelle
I fall; appalled, I pale
at the aphotic zone.
Noting the ant lion's dangerous
funnels at the foot of the musk thistle
and the wondrous morning lights
on the leafy spurge and the yet damp spiny clotbur
I am at home with noxious weeds
and seconds closer
to my aphelion.

It storms in the high needles and crowns;
heavy flakes smother boughs and feelings.
Thoughts weigh downward under the world's
first snow on thirsty pumice and dying roots.
Too soon again spring and summer slipped past
like feral twins and fled to hibernate.

Fall's distant desert, bright with expectant qualities,
informed the anxious old man
and the awed infant within.
The cycle ended—another starts again.

I can't recall why I wandered off between
boulders and vastness (my playground when
I was young) a transient homunculus
fatally shaped but perfectly mirrored in
the eye glint of a thousand watching lizards,
abiding there since ancient waters.

Basking in the late rays, a poor mimic of
instinctive lizard, I gave up grand hopes
for fellow kind and for myself and dropped it
all with my tears and spit amid husks and
rinds the marmots left behind.

Between talus fragments left cracked from the face
ten million years, washed under the bitter-brush

all singing from that chaparral whose yellow flowers
remain until the very end, until aspens quake
in their own white bark and winter quail fly.

In this very parched earth,
look for blood.
Other than my own,
I see no other flesh here.
The desert flower
purple blooms
from the long buried seed.
Take stock of your weapons.
Keep eyes on the weather.
Everyone has left.
Insects with their molted casks
shuddering in the blue wind.
one black raindrop
on a smiling stone.
Blood of sacrifice
black in the wasted air,
the silver moon,
the color of bone.
T'is the luna of
someone's fingernail.

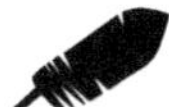

It snowed
just as the geese knew it would, just
as they told me it would.
The low ceiling keeps them down
waiting for stars.

A muffled jet pries around the higher clouds
looking for the ground, flies up in full sun
across a boiling dazzle on shocked wings, on things
invisible, visible in dials; bright dials dull
war dials and the digital displays.
Their phosphorescence rises—cautious eyes—computerized
search indices, seek peaks, track vessels
in the seas, timbered passes at timber-line
penetrate this the first snow below the heavy nimbus line.
Snowing slightly now where radar combs
my morning hair.

In falling air, geese confer
and children laugh, dance in dirty streets
throw gritty snowballs in the thousand streets
that lead to school halls and playground paths
shown picture-perfect in ozone zones
circling in oscilloscopes the green line sweeps.

Geese, moving now, signaling:
nerves waken in the scanning,
lungs quicken the calling, all flying now.
The coffee's hot, the cream, the calcium,
strontium-ninety, follows to the bone sponge
and plutonium works and worms
in the swarming silence television
intrudes upon.
Inured, the clever isotopes endure.
How this hiding sun depresses with the first snow pack!

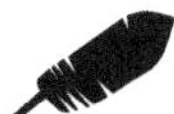

The iron rooster fitfully
squeals in the intermittence.
In the distance the grey horse
stands on three hooves.
A crocus opens
at moon's crescendo.
Between blood and seed,
I brought you panting
to the stress of your month.

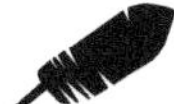

It was winter, then summer, the spring lost
between the white powders of frost and drought.
Our patient bison await the changes,
for all the posts to rot
and the barbed wire to fall to rust.
I sharpen my sword at the world's edge
and learn the language of gibbons
The ape stains in my clothes hang in the closet.

Estranged, endangered, angered
with the unpronounceable
perception at the door,
I am too much with myself
and the mountain gorilla.

Now close enough to taste the shadow,
but far from close enough.
Now, close enough for the fine detail, the
florid tile and the wrought iron eye
in the mortuary wall,
far enough for an overview
at this fragrant flood-plain,
this nubile field with freckled blossoms
each with its legs outspread.

What of the unborn, if nature be undone?
Is it possible to ask and is the answer
merely a lament and a question
turned upon itself,
a dying salamander?

I've just visited the floodgates
whelmed over the avalanche
of the most durable granite
and andesite and found the
most angry river god
who speaks violently
with his rumble of restless rolling boulders,
until settling into meander, switchbacks, and
private cirques along his way.
Should I stop now to propitiate this
god whose name is unpronounceable?
He can only be adored by
sacrifice lest he become exhausted.
I have not yet made ready my own sacrifice.

Moments, hours, days,
filaments burn in last rays.
Spiders at the headland,
a bleak land where solitary
stones haunt the loneliness:
the stones which were left standing,
one day, of a sudden, when earth washed away.

Hatred and malice, a cyan sky, the basalt phallus—
evening red never sated, then, startled among
stalagmites, numb and horrified—with our feeble torches,
we emerged beautifully scarified and awake to the bird's
contradictions in the boiling sky, the sky, the sky.
How quick the clouds westering past sunny aeries
where dark eagles angle out in raking light over
stunning estuaries.

Stones yield to the down wear
as the horned one stands forlorn in the line of sight.
Seas, encroach and crowd the overhang.
Even yet, shamans flay sacred things
from archaic night
again and again.
I recommend the three low notes piped
on consoling bones to coax the nervous herds.

Failure—the fact, alone:
an old clock wound too tight.
Do you think I'm going away?
I'm not.

I'm just coming back.
But for the spiders, this could have been
a love song.

This has been a vacant place,
since that silent crew in hard hats
and with great machines for moving earth,
came one day to remove the dead.
the multilingual jay sifts the earth for its valuables,
but nothing remains. Headstones...holes.
The earth for all its worth,
seems as far away as the moon.

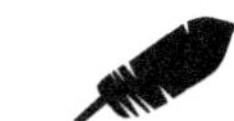

Kitchen middens

With a hollow cough from within the sallow window,
I have gathered the two dirty curtains
and tied them in a knot
at the day's end,
and then I drown in my own blood,
as I do each night.
By the refuse, heaped with countless excuses,
my life's detritus,
you can tell I was here.

My sly pariah
stands by waiting
for whatever remains of me,
feeds upon bloody fringes
of human frailty.
And I?
I eat stilbestrol meat
dioxin treat in mayonnaise.
I bless this rock
where the owl shits
cleaner than
the sandwich.

Sorrowful moon!
Ever-present moon
Hanging there full-faced,
pockmarked, say rather, faun-spotted
deer of my ancestors:
or a moon sliver thin as the shrill
creature cry from the limitless night.

I sleep as the new era dreams in the magma.

Nature, you counsel,
provides not consolation:
the beast lurks there as well,
fanged, slavering and unsouled.
But the strike of hawk,
abandoned fawn,
relate to a necessity,
a purpose self-regulated,
devoid of gesture.
Beside mankind's practiced sport
of butchery, calculated pain.
Nature who deals in her measure of daily death,
offers to me a gentler face.

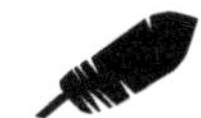

My Thoughts are Shrouded

My thoughts are shrouded by an estranged alphabet
seen before, wrought by few in any age.
Again the water has subsided, giving way to
crazed mud lands.

My thoughts are crowded with linear scatterings and
stranded mollusks, cracks leading to the very farthest ending,
leading as if we had followed in a previous time to a vivid future,
livid beyond shapes and tints.
Mornings and evenings and living waters return the waves'
spiral moments in comers, coming back, covering nervous
dust with random movements, the fingers of the first waters
with brine and life held in the preferred palm of the sea,
with a gift of language that swells with kelp and ocean odors,
and flashing hatchlings, bream, the squirming gold, the furrowed
color, green, coming in wave after wave to high water marks.
And the clever magpie eyeing the open paunch
teetering at the brink.

I detect something; in the tranquility between storms, a shiver.
The off-axis perturbation, between our prayers to the huge male
god stiffened like a stallion across the sky.
The great wanton body seen from any distance
as subjective lines connecting stars like galaxies.

Arriving back from the weeping source, now nearly dry,
cracks show in the unity, as we stand alone in ruined pavilions
recently vacated, or alone, just standing there, in the middle
of a sentence without an end.
Or better yet, alone with fractured lava the color of manganese.
Amethystine quartz in glowing stria:
Mauve moves with the moon,
jet black and silver lines in psilomelane.

Anesthetized in the yellow cliffs is the seas guilt
deepening with ignorance,
only to grow wider in the latter years
ripped with indifference from the long rain.

I realize language is dying with the earth.

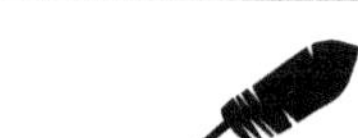

October has returned with my
shoes yet filled with the bones
of my own feet.
The young prairie falcon has become a memory.
Nearby in a stiff breeze swans
riding the whale road on another high wind,
but die here along the way of
Asian cholera year after year
after their too long flight from Patagonia.

Spirals of birth tell of time,
years fail and at the end
far boulders shroud the stunted junipers
where the disconsolate lion
shepherds its mule deer.

Say good morning to the blood lined cloud.
O how my mother haunts me. O her sad life!
Say good morning to the rouge
and petroglyphs on the wizened lava's
old language of tears.

Preachy finches
who bear right down on things
over and over,
who know you by your own words
and the sound of your laughter.
Itinerant clouds in an exiled sky
that single sail of great longing
obscured horizon barely in human sight
which is within pure reason why I feel so alone,
A subject ardently studied by
my favorite phenomenologist
who also brought his critique
to bear on the weather.
But when the moon came,
All that was left of my fragmented memories
were the caskets moored against the moonlight
which moved across a luminous river
of phosphorescent glass.

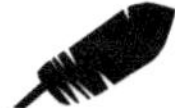

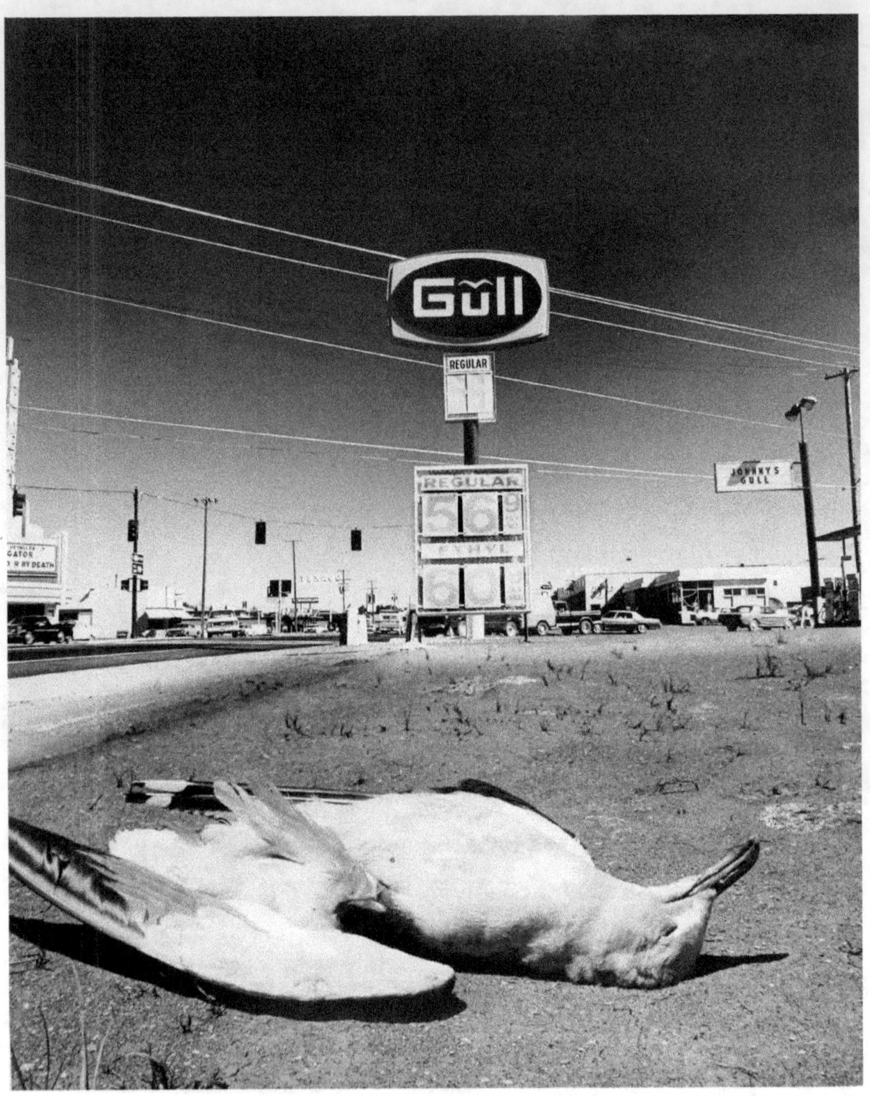
GULL
REGULAR
REGULAR
JOHNNYS GULL

Passing overhead almost endlessly, so closely
I could see them watching me—
clouds of gulls in migration
to the ocean, flight after flight,
no end to gulls.
My childhood's strong impression; lying in awe of
the herring gulls in their flights to the sea.

Now the gulls are fewer and spoiled, greedy and somehow
malign, roost in shopping centers atop bullet shaped
mercury vapor parking lot lights, play the vulture,
swarm, beg for candy wrappers, for some flimsy hamburger rinds.

Some, sickened, wait at the curbs to die—sad feathers.
Some cruise the city dump, wheeling chaotically, unsteadily,
finding Christ knows what at the sump
in those dangerous barrels.

I remember those steady flights; the staggered formations
the V's and W's shaped like grand and moving words
written on the sky.

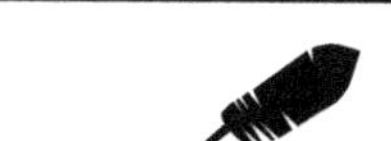

Returning to the high aerie
from distant curves of sky and world
eagles soar, vultures float in rose light;
shadows carpet escarpment, bridging dark
rocks and connecting shades build the night.

Running fast between swell and wash
my foot prints close upon me;
ancient bones between the varves guide me,
but I seek and search and never find
where love begins and horizon ends.

My tracks are running deep over loam and flint
over fine rare earths, that in a hot flux melt
make the lens that can focus on eternity.
In the sand I draw a dog; old in tooth
ranging wide, my coyote comforts me.

Spring
dawn brings down mist—how good it feels
to hear the first thrilling songs
sung across the fields—this damp fragrant hay
a wide gobbly nest of pink mouths upraised awaiting
maternal shadows flying back with morning meals
of tasty bugs in tireless bills.

But today this noisy spray plane comes instead—
a relentless yellow monoplane
that stuns my head and flies close enough to grin,
throws a hand sign so arrogantly—full throttle on the
turns—then kills the dawn and my avocado tree
and feeds gaping chicks 2-4D.

Now the killdeer a heroic and skilled deceiver
strikes its tricolors, feigns lame injury fluttering
to another field crying
kill me—kill me
kill me—kill me

This dreadful deathly odor, this falling mist sinking in
makes the dangerous ape rise up in me;
These silent birds—
a stinking sin.
it strikes me
it strikes me
it strikes me

The river that always could give up
bass and catfish
was a dry grave
and had been for years.

I kept my chin straight ahead and hoped
the past wouldn't recognize me.
I uttered nothing aloud about rotting stumps
on the overgraze.

I watch where I step in this sprawling country
where a pair of sun glasses might disappear
as though they never existed.
Oriented for legend, they hurry on, flimsily.

A cloud has descended like a hanging drift net,
thirty miles long.
To the south a purse seine surrounds
the unseen north over the Cascades.

Like a listing trawler leaking oil
is a stratonimbus
stretching all the way to
ultima Thule.

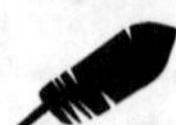

The moon blunders up
intrudes across the silver hills
and lights the sides of heaven:
catches the dreaming dog between
muffled yelps and running spasms
his phantom rabbit down
the limbic hole, safe again
another night.

Old dog eyes no longer dreaming
well up with phosphorescent moons
and atavistic fevers.
Is it the starting shadow
I see dart from the side
then waver and vanish among
dim fear forms
to reappear in the corner of
my other eye?

There, the dog is running close
in his relentless lope
hot on a trail of fright
the figures slipping out in nacreous light:
Running, running till the moon
is hounded
to the horizon's darkest night.

Mount St. Helens

And the sun passes the day moon,
clouds coast with ponderous meanings.
This great light which I see for an instant, this
wondrous sign swaying before the storm and the petals
born upon the wistful river.

This was the day before the obscure wind,
taste of ash,
and the odor of darkness
where at last the year revealed its mission,
ushering a new age.
At the snowline
where the crater widened
and the smoke beckoned the unwary,
eagles took flight, sailed beyond the tilted shadow
and old dreamers
awakened to howl with maddened dogs
and now to the groan of a great forest falling.
I have come to witness the evening, the men in flight
and the extinguished moon.

The weak light searches out the wrinkled shore,
touching once the stones, settles back
against indifferent slopes and dies.
Laconic question sung upon a lake
marks the time of grebes
and little falling back at zero gradient.

The evidence is certain;
at the spin off we were part of that detonation,
distant, yet roaring in eternity.
Some believe that just beyond this upright stone
the future starts.

Is this different from
our hypothesis of altered form?

The work being finished, destruction followed.
Was it here our diviner read the random alignments
and foretold the contamination of a notion, of a nation, of an ocean?
A race which walks upright, walls up whole mountain chains,
turns miraculous springs fetid, takes on an onus too great to bear.
A rain of ash from deep within the overburden,
from the under burden a dissonant voice
indistinguishable from voice, but
something like a snore, more like
something miserable.
Rumor vents from the many fumaroles;
gas is sulfurous anger, ash grey as dust to dust.

I find, in the morning bones that man is nature
and that man is wanton and beyond nature.
With the fish I flounder in reconciliation.
Note the thunder! Hordes are packing
and can be heard coming this way;
tremors bring abrupt belching.
Scoria and lava bombs the size of whales
fall among their own fatal distortions... the black plume!

Lord of wasps, fly with us!
Lord of scorpions, crawl with us!
Correct our deceptive dialect.
Insistence is dissidence, but a protest too feeble.
My cry is a whisper in this twittering cave;
its echo shocks me,
and the bugling of extinct mastodons
trumpet from the stress and stria.

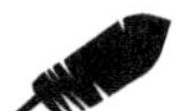

That I should consume nothing other than sand
I would dress myself in stones.
With a sky heavy with white boulders
my own words fall as rocks
as I rave and accumulate between these varves
which once were estuaries
as bright as primordial sun.
But now my eagles cry.
My life is now aggregate
visited more than once by the wandering dust devil,
an evil I hear say no.
I had promised to sing praises to forests.
But what now?
Only a cry in this night without sleepers.
This eternal no, an interminable no.
Was there ever a yes from some deity unknown
without a niche in this land of cinerary ash
among millions unknown?

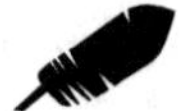

The universal law beyond understanding
picture the silver:
in the Danish museum, the Celtic hag
slits a throat not her own
over the greedy Gundestrup Cauldron,
divining the future,
just as now Roberta Bleakney
reads tea leaves to
bloodshot peonies.
Now then, don't you see how oblivious death
shrouds itself in futurity,
as the universe fills itself with time?

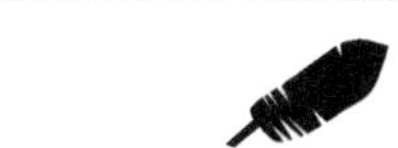

Through evening light eagles soar from distant curves
of sky and world.
Vultures tire at last and fall
to those high aeries which merge
with escarpment shadows on black boulders with
almond eyes set deep in basalt skin
watching with mineral stare horizon's reflected light.
This is Oregon; it is dark; it is night.

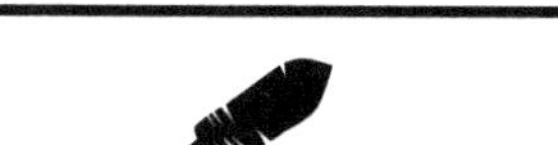

These uterine anemones,
so sensitive, so cervical,
responsive buttons to teasing touch,
they withdraw, ejaculate, cinching up.

I've become more careful where I step when
sleep-walking at the womb, returning to my birth.

Tomorrow evening we shall chart
the night hawks' velocities on dying horizons;
Tomorrow evening, I shall show you rhythms at the verticies
giant circles at the crossings.

We flame at the windy sweep,
burning straight out with bending trees.
Will grows in the presence of steepness;
burning orange trees ignite
as we wait at the incline, becoming stronger.

We are seekers of buds
the adventitious marks on stems;
desires blaze at stem ends.
Spring is long way off,
but already signs can be seen:
signs when clouds burn off and water boils.

Wind teaches: birds on the wind are voices teaching
us signs; hear voices of water on rock,
the surges in seasons, surfeit of water, then
the dearth, a death in dust.

Wind and water are lessons taught in strata;
varves are the pages in situ where wind gathers its dust
in devils and strikes dark motions on the water.
And at the eroded reaches
we've become connoisseurs of the ossified,
at peace with their smiles,
at home with bones.
We look for them.

Wind on water, water on stone.
We lose our fear; reduce our needs
and vulnerabilities.

With its signature inscribed upon the clavicle,
the worm informs us that no harm has come
to those who lived here.

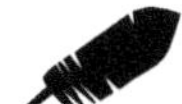

This shuddering night so close around me
how was it I came to this, these firm hills
the shape of breasts, this soft phosphorus
that reveals the lost beasts trapped in amber
or the antique evil yet present in the green shale?

The constellations take up their positions
with the awed ancestors.
I clear away the sand
and beckon to the star light.

I examine these hills built of violence and frozen turmoil,
the pale dream a blackbird cipher in a pressed leaf.

I have come for this rhythmic wind,
its low moaning, tears of hysteria—
this stone with wonder inside
shining secretly like a third eye.
—Sharks teeth!
And above, I watch the thrilling sunsets on the
trillion worlds at midnight.

Thready crickets—chitin scrapes from smaller spaces, emerging
bats squint tiny cries and owls' eyes dilate. The evening
in fixity, the cat considers the invisible finch.
The century's last eclipse, the bitten sun that measures
our decades, sensitive in the looming penumbra, ill at ease
in the umbra.

Thinking little of our unconsidered sins, little is what
you thought it was; of what you thought little remains for
fear is trapped in our basements, cast in concrete.
All men thinking, think the same thing.

At the umbra, scree from stirred embers where our crazed teeth
in signs reveal our return to the drone drum
and clap sticks on the morning of the ninth moon,
so that stiff dance the emu taught us
a post millennial event no doubt.

A meeting has been called, a summit, to buy time,
but the houses are ordered to be boarded up and all have
fled the blown down forest except one devil found,
he the unknown one, lying faceless in sterile ash
at the farthest end of his tracks, like the dried centipede
curled into a question.

Take care. The dark devil approaches, his face in painted
stripes, chalk white dances as red-eyed flies in a dervish wind,
his flies bred in monstrous middens in this age of starvation.

This song cannot be taught unless you know it.
Unless you've heard it, this song cannot be heard.

This is the pain of the earliest years, looking into rooms
finding no one, looking for my mother in all women,
sensing the future catastrophe in the sliced grapefruit,
hearing my voice in desolated gorges,
grappling with summits and brinks,
deciphering articulate stones,
translating blue poems of lightning,
seeing my own face in that viscera on a receding shore,
rocking, cradling death in my arms like a newborn.

This is a paean to the rising sun
drenching its dark planet with great surprise
with the perched, ancient-eyed osprey waiting
for the black wave down under
to become a beautiful flounder.

The most important hour in my life spins
in my hand then falls quiet under the yet
visible death star.
My sky becomes blue.
This is the light of tremulous amber.

Angels in basalt succumb to the bright vibration
Where the god of vengeance visits this and each morning
with tremendous anger.

I commend myself yonder to the water,
to the yellow shimmer under lazy elms.
Morning, with full straight light,
for the very first time, finds the official doctrine
which supports seven massive lies.

(Perfumed wind penetrates impenetrable thoughts)

An arctic tear has become a single yellow crystal
as beautiful as, as tragic as, the long isolation
and continuing absence when I speak to the shaman and
call into reality his most hated dream.

Then traveling from the dream, but not too far,
life measured by the dream is life endlessly falling
to the rocks below or floating above the public ruin,
the ephemeral metal, amoral and lethal, of
defeated people; the long pink cicatrice
stretches out across our lives in this endless
red desert.

Yes, with wild dreams, with fever,
where I stand is my place in the dawn.

Those stones of great bearing
dignify the farscape
watching, holding their secrets
until their time
for inheritance.

What does this time declare
beyond the gulls worried mewing?
What does the crazed stone
say at midday in this dry age
when rain seldom falls
to wash the tears we shed
at the boundary stones,
when not long ago (you know where) the blazing god
in his own lava snorted forth our new age?

We shall admire the fumaroles
where the gods feast to surfeit with renewed gluttony
beyond belief or relief, a groaning and grappling.
Once more with another failed dream
that summons bones
blows rose powder and the rose to powder
with little hope in reservation of the tanks
we bury, past caring, in scant grass.

And I myself am giving
great attention to the cleverness of the ant lion
in this worldwide Sahara
of the post steady state.

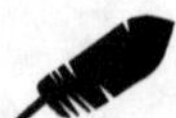

Crowded at the Edge

Book 2

The Ancient World, Archeology & History

Crowded to the edge of sunset,
this dry world is a worried frown
scorched upon the furrowed brain.

From far beyond that wild, leaning tree
blows the blue wind unraveling
the white hair of the same goddess
who doles out to each of us
our portions of time.

Upon every word hang the hours,
on the trees, on remembered fields
and by the threads of dismembered
evenings.

I speak to you and to the old men
who sprinkle prayers
and cornmeal upon rattlesnakes
and to those who have risked much danger,
who, in the end, have fallen in love
with whales.
I invite you to walk with me
through the ever present bones
of our dead selves.

An age waning, an age gaining dust.
I gather it about me

and cast it to the wind's awesome song
and we find direction.

In the long, long ago, in the down wear
in the presence of the granite sibyl,
whose features harden with every sunset
I stopped to put on my most hideous mask
with its crow's feet grown about the eyes.

Without beginning, universe without end,
and this minimal world, as usual ruled by criminals,
the wind shifts toward us completing the symbol and syntax,
and we are what we are.

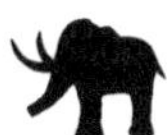

Bird on an ancient bough
with eyes age-old and practical,
watchful and waiting,
waiting for the era to complete.
When withered corpses hang from
poles and pines and overpasses,
paunches blown and leaking on the pavement,
and your poor body among them, and
there is Pica—to pick out your bonny blue een.

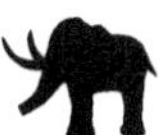

A child is seen as ball of flesh born of loving woman,
but then a crippled king uncovering the basket may find
a thousand perfect baby boys—
all Buddhas reborn.

But now there is silence in the wilderness.
There, did you see? All the voles have fled away through sunless grass
the motionless heron is teaching me meditation.
My hair turns to white plumes.
There ravenous hogs are set foraging in the emus' last holdout.
Now I'm an emu immaculate in my shell dreaming centuries of grass
flightless under impeccable skies.
And you? I've seen your plumes show
when the wind comes up.
Now the egrets have abandoned their old savannahs
for the new world, too late—
have flown in long airy flocks across the whole Atlantic
in search of elephants, too late.

I regress, I'm regrowing gill slits.
Memory of it traces astral paths:
remains of old salinities on the tongue,
external sight and sound watched inward with internal eye
heard within the internal ear
through cochlea canals
the semicircular chamber

as numb notochords perfected
during the grand cycles
finally swim away as sharks.

Celtic lurs,
the million moans from the sad fields,
harpsichords and Sumerian bells,
and the last shouts from a smoking ridge,
sounds from the long chambers,
the heavy swell tumbling autoliths
all brush cilia cells.
And once again Shiva and Parvati couple
and dance upon the child of ignorance.

I should be joyful but instead I feel this terrible dread
so many waves have fallen and I'll never know.
We hold on at the steady angle out to the green wave.
Perhaps it was here on a shore very much like this one
we were once some wondrous sort of lizard searching
along the litora for the perfect gizzard stone.
A brighter sun sparked our emerald eyes,
dark green waves welled,
each an overwhelming urge
surged in dissolution, broke back
gathered and reared again, darker than before;
eight more, than the ninth, swelling even stronger.

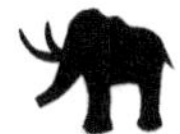

Do you remember Dionysius?
The sail made of the living vine grown to keel,
his boat becalmed on an inland sea rocked in the eyes of
plaintive herring gulls crying to distance.

Hero became Sabasius of the green ocean sun dreaming, rocking.
Slowly wheeling with weeping gulls over dark waters
which meet the firmament at the uncharted opposites
joined at unknown peripheries,
merged black galactic sky,
who became night God:
the fires burning on the shores.

Pray Dionysius, as he prayed upon his knees
In the world's first nave.
Drank from the first wine squeezed from the living arbor.
Lapping.
Lapping night, slept the sleep of death.
Adrift without direction,
without land fall,
without end.
For you we paint this stone red as wine,
red blood of resurrection.
Genuflux to migrations,
attend swan songs.
Heed the gulls.
Sing with waves.

We remember those sons and daughters who built and
tended the fires to guide you home.
Your seeds, washed ashore, become again a living vine.

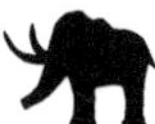

How now brown cloud
now that the mastodons have turned over in their graves.
No grass left where they've been.
Those men, those men, stay away from them
they will make reliquaries from mammoth bones,
make tents of the tusks, taken from your
prognathous jaws, taking all, as always.
Your latter day cousins are still afoot, for a time at least.
Craftsmen make ornaments, glorifying the misdeeds of men,
profiteering at their expense.
Ancient footpaths crisscrossing all of Asia,
now less trodden.
Weary legs like falling trees lumber
under these low brown clouds.

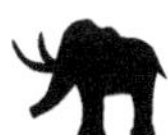

Can you hear the voices in the long grave chambers
the grunting and plunging
of slaughtered horses crying out
and all the moaning afterward?
And the business of crows
is as audible as
gas blowing from distended paunches,
as it all happened before,
when the Hyksos drove their chariots
across the water?

Red dawn, bloody dusk,
It was the ravens at yet another massive meal.

All history is on raven's tongues
wisdom natural about their eyes.
The word begun in blood shows the way,
and bones witness.

Odin's ravens perch atop the picture stones in Gottland.
Words written on patient stones were first sketched
in blood, clouds, and thunder. Ages rage.

Thought and Memory, Odin's Huginn and Muninn, forever buried.
All knowledge is at peace with the ground
where Nidhogg gnaws at Yggdrasil, the world tree,
gnawed long before the serpent was loosed in Eden.

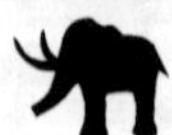

And I find myself coming back,
find you beside me on the berms,
And parapets stumbling through the desolation.
Cracks heaved by fervent grass.
Purple flowers push aside
the trash where the lowest of the living crawled,
buried where they fell, lie in boxes by the wall:
watered by the eaves,
penstemon, gentian, lupine.
One flattened forget-me-not
pressed between the sentences.
Shadows overthrow the bones in boxes.
Under stairways crawls the layered trail, the trilobite.
Leaf compress in the tonnage of things
at the landing where our laughter spilled.
This fossil stairway rising on the wall
where we might hide our books.
Everything is left to you and me,
and I think we are leaving too,
looking for the wolf to suck;
searching for a place to throw the dragon's teeth,
to find a new monument for hope,
to found a new city.

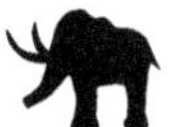

These three poems, Cruel Cruel, Breath—animal—anima—asthma, and Huichol Women, are excerpts from writing done while staying with the Huichol Indians near Jalisco

Cruel, cruel,
this hide is monstrous,
is magnified;
skin of relentless rivers,
where torrents grind,
cut the fissures deeper,
its bluffs, its caves, are eyes,
abut the far front;
it turns to watch itself,
its own savage face;
this cliff confronts the absolute,
itself in breathlessness;
this sun, its planets in phasing grasp,
this moon, our moon in shaman's prayer.
Our lives are gripped where
naked peaks grow the Tree of Wind.
The jaguar coughs in answer to the
the shamans prayers
where ravines plunge
to the jungle's tangled hair
where preach the priests of dark holes
and secret earth, see light in vision,
entranced, hear voices teach, calling,
reach Wirikuta, ancestral hole
below the skin.

No wires mar the sky,
nowhere are there roads to nowhere
at the sacred navel
here in the middle of
the massif, the world-womb
of Sierra Madre Occidental

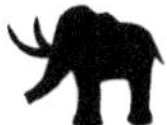

Breath—animal—anima—asthma
the spider-shaman
asphyxiates
overseen by Oversoul as Vulture watches.
Vulture is black
red wattled
hunkering by the open crack
waiting for those who live
to edge closer and closer
to fall through finally,
as do we all.
On the way to Wirikuta
the arroyo eats the path.

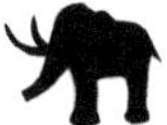

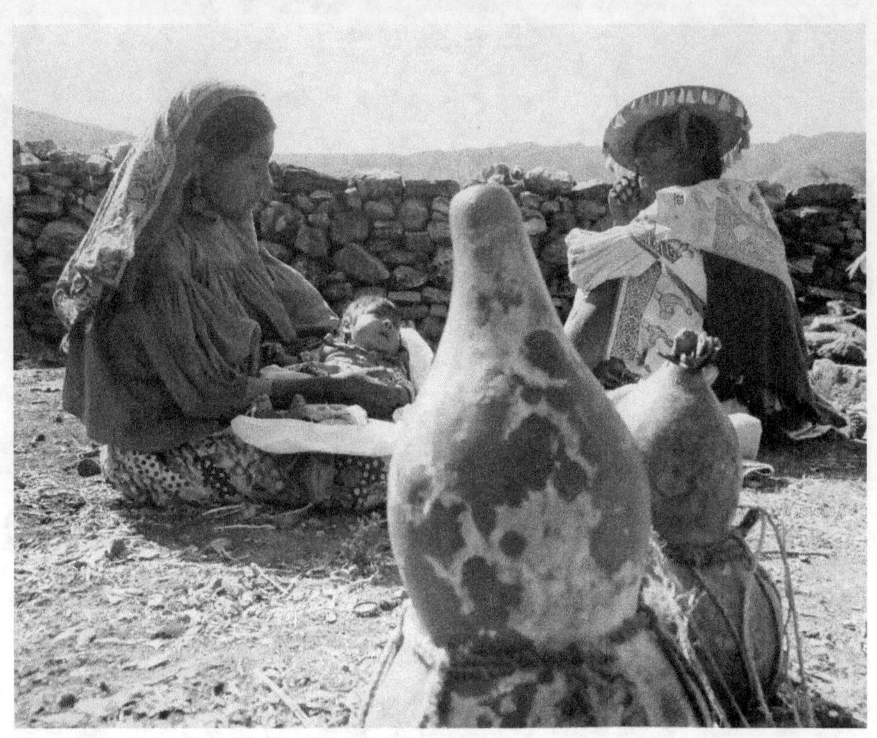

Huichol Women

On this hill of grief, seated by the ever-open crack
women work with eyes averted from the writhing coil
deeply felt obscurely seen half remembered from a dream
conjured from a scream.

On this hill of air, webs float that spiders weave.
Daughters of despair search the hill of air find the
dust of names of those who never lived their second year, remember
dust of bones in winter air
where it ends no one knows, but where it ends
there is no end to dust in endlessness.

Expectant silks fall in breathlessness
pick the figs, sweeter than the winter breeze, on this hill
of grief in this orchard of despair
twilight comes on soft owl's wing
our shadows cast out to nothingness
in deep perspective extenuate
outward into endlessness.

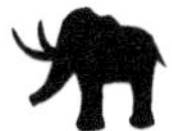

Shiva's Necklace

Deep wallows
and washes
three great strides
as I sleep.

I feel the desert wind erodes my
skeletal ribs.
Three sunken pits Shiva kept.
Three steps at the deer trail
dark Vishnu crept—*mriganca.*

And now the moon springs up fawn-spotted
mriga dhara.
Its brightness is dharma.
For as long as the sun,
my juniper,
my banyan,
hangs upside down
roots point up.
This Bodi tree
the tiger leapt
and these grazing clouds
cows Krishna kept.
My turned down mouth
the cave where Kali wept

How empty my heart where sweet Parvati
in soft abandon slept
and the moon's yellow halo grows antlered
silk at the edges,
hari-hari, Shiva's necklace.
When the moon nudges, I am *mrigaiu.*

I have sought; I seek; I speak
under the hunters moon.
Pour me more clouds,
fast streaming, like these,
like buttermilk.

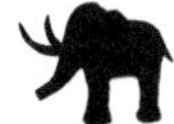

Do I seek? Have I sought the ineffable as I've come across
the interrogative rune carved so lightly into this indelible ruin
where I've attempted translation
mounted high over clouds, orange fringed, tinged with violence,
farther and wider, only to catch myself with everything amiss,
my feet dangling over an abyss?

Do I ask? Are those ships of the future listing with limp hausers
and dragging anchors, all sailors missing mooring
or destination?
All questions without answers?

Ships of the torn rivage, where not one woman
waves farewell, not one kiss to tell?
Is this the time; the hour of the hound and far calling goose?
The whale's long song that no one hears?
Is this the time? The incessant tide
against which all things human are measured:
The carbolic acid and tri-nitro-toluene
Of great nuclear mega-dream now at phenol eventide?

But listen! Here is Snottor "on mode," waiting this long time,
Snottor waiting at the tide pool.
Look down at my simian visage, wavering among the anemones,
in fright as if they were waving among enemies.

And little more in that frail image
but ephemeral age.
between thumb and forefinger, aching for a trigger.
There, Snottor, the wise, points his finger at you and me,
for it was I who consumed a forest,
and you who helped me excavate those meandering trenches
septic ditches which filled with friends who looked like
too thin gods carved rose veined from white marble with limbs akimbo.
Gods all badly used and thrown away, but those were people
and without people there exist no gods.

Teach me runes; I shall keep them deep
then mount them in the gneiss, pale andesite, black basalt.
I want the rune that says scandal and those that signify death of earth.
I shall be inseparable from stone and merge with it
and stillness will become our fast friend with idled hands.

At last, like the most patient astronomer,
I observe the ten pale moons again rising from my fingernails.

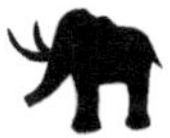

In a darkening sky, loaded with voice, geese fall with leaves,
blackening, call to the dim fields, blanketing,
black with white mosaic faces patterning the mud lands,
await another phasing moon,
take the offered food from the proffered land
during the season I regret.
Snow gathers at the summit, the felled trees,
under forgetful drifts and bones
asleep under the quiet listing of cliffs
and a wind which is in itself undeniable
with all its possibilities of time and terrain
and the end of all possibilities
carried with it, the shift of crystals.
Tits twitter from their occasional bushes
and after a time stones capsize—eventually.

What is this?
A vision shadowed in stone, or this rock in essence crated
in angles from flesh, or this sea within me, rises within me,
drains the features away.
And what are these geese darkening the rye, settling,
bringing tired memories from the north filling my admiring eyes?

Falling with them, falling back, I await a leaping forth,
my blood, a pounding froth, my ghosts and chasing them
I lurch through memories in pursuit of autumn's naked forests and bare
tamaracks
where the wandering elk bellow to their cows in a steaming dawn.

A sigh of relief in a gathering of scavengers; we are sifting
the earth for rat's teeth, on the lookout for the Ancestor.
I well remember who we are.

We are the ones who hold earth hostage in streets of blaspheme and
chanting.
In streets named in self-esteem we riot
calling out for the Ancestor.

—Ow! Cry of the new born.
—The ones who knew told us, the shadow struck the birthing place
so the child was slain, so the watchers told us,
because of the shadow the retinue was formed,
our belongings gathered, longings scattered, fires quenched;
our tents pitched and rolled we left
that regrettable place in sniggering shadows.

Nodding off, sleeping snatches, digging at the itch,
now I've forgotten where I was in that long caravan in that long time
we trudged from dream to dream on a plain so vast its end was the
world's edge.

Say, do you remember what those words were—realize what
birds say to December morning, the phrases rise,
signal to the size and color of the morning
A beautiful place to be, I see their faces among oblong stones,
yours belongs among them;
I hear ancestral laughter roll down
the gradient, transient bells,
and your silken whisper at the intermittent fires
with our evening meals
and the black wine's delicious kisses.

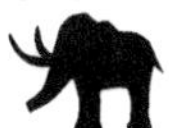

During a dearth, unwatered scant grass
brings forth the century's locusts:
god's eye at high noon, obsidian,
focused on fuming earth;
the deity's bewildering eye withers
yet another thready heart
set atop the Toltec's capstone.

At birth the greatest journey.
How we regret eternity,
in a dry wind, in an instant,
the sand swept from the stone.
The squalling infant crying out the first word
is cut loose in yawning infinity.

This desert dreams in expectation of water.
This mind dreams expecting the desert,
the cause of which I mean to know
before my guilt has increased
for in dire need the wolves made off
with the bison hide, illustrated,
painted with the truest account
of the destruction drama.

This is the city of which I seldom speak,
deadly of air, doomed to looming alleys,
asbestos sifting in darkening quietude

with doors opening, giving out on sordid shadows,
steel doors closing on the trash.
The muffled flush of the abortionist's stained porcelains
cigarette butts moored to the high tide marks in our filthy basins
our fish-eyed fetuses float past the grinning steel grates,
blind in benzene.

There! I flee to the desert and conjured clouds.

But we must hurry on
before the colors cease from the desperate lateness.
Within this viscous twilight, this same thin kitten,
in its evening visitations at the loading ramp,
may be seen again.

Golden elytra, scarab of greatest beauty,
pushes the sun across the sky to awaken human kind.
We meanwhile take aggressive steps at the trend line
with the laws rolled back for free enterprise.
We stand behind the learning curve and ask
what is the cumulative effect on these rancid sloughs,
in a larger sense, because the trees are gone,
because the bees have gone?
From afar, Isis, sounding her crux, takes full measure.

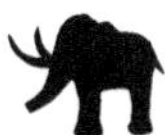

In the frozen earth beside me sleeps a Viking. I love her grey hair.
The determined statues of Cernunnos face eternity, determining
as we face the music and the grudge born to us on the
seething sky, as this night with blackened fingers nudges us—
our lives died in our own arms.

Ages in decline, contagious rages in descending
line and the mountain becomes alert to our ephemeral footfall.
We kneel and succumb in fallout at the outfall
where we poured our verses from splendid amphorae,
toasted hope with the dark wines of the Pyrenees
caught the festival of fish, marched in single purpose
with processional lamps lighting our way
through the rostrums and altars.
Our memories in urns. Our ashes spill among the ruins
where our ancestors were carried home draped on their shields,
where the jaguar is executed for nothing more than his rosettes.

From blood beyond the boulders the universal rose opens once more
with great satisfaction.
But the rising earth escapes me, the meaning, the riddle
of the white fronted geese. Sibyls frail sockets watch the eternal,
the slow gyration, the endless possibility, plenitude, the goddess
undressed in the unimaginable infinitude.

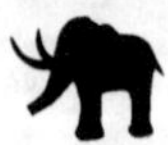

Now the land has finished squirming and the sun is set swarming
with slaughtered porpoises.
A young man with an iron rod strikes rhythmically upon the fire escape.
A bus from California disgorges and everyone recovers,
gathers luggage and stands in line.
As usual another cat has followed me home
begging for nothing other than life.

I have honored and photographed
the last eclipse of the century and in my short time
I have witnessed this mountain worn down to fine sand.
As night gathers its brilliance, dust gives up its souls.
I adjust this golden mask fashioned by my ancestors.

Home again,
I growl to the darkness.
My combative tom has returned
with an exquisite cyst
on his jowl.

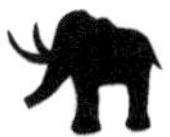

In the morning
after a short sleep
my head emerges
as a large tumulus filled with
slaughtered horses and a quite a few long dead
relatives.

I think I must have been there
to bury them to have carried them
down to dark earth with careful ritual
and bright felt ornament and
Theocritus' strong voice of bronze at the instant
of human sacrifice to the savage Asian
goddess.

All has stayed then long time
in permafrost covered by these alluvial gravels,
where they, uncovered, were discovered
this morning when my eyes re-opened.

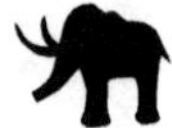

Once more night is crucified across another mountain side,
another day past, the last before the enormous dawn
as we wait within the starkness, the tidal altitude reaches
the height of our reckless experiment.
Our urbane audience or these listening baboons
all simians in full display in crimson estrous,
as legible bands of geese in a long stanza rise in the chronological
sky as a phrase in exhortation to the ancient army silent in loss and
failure.
Curling in clouds silver lined like Baroque pearls
with mauve pouring through to the burnt grass.
The pulse of the Huichol's great fig tree
is beating in my left wrist.
As the crack widens, fate is sealed in the sign,
the smoking tongue or in this
deep music from the mountain.
Who was I in a time the river
cut found its level in these eroded stones?
When we rested at midday
with no thought of cover, hidden from the heat with the pride and
their prey, who were we?
Of the grandest ages, the most famous storms,
the most illustrious summers are gathered here and summarized.
All meanings wait in origins,
in the stain of umber under the evidence, in this dust, odor of blood,
in this sign of murder under the ocher, with far sepulcher
stratified in mystery or yonder in that plowed grave land
rolled out against the hills which look just like hills
but with something wrong with them.

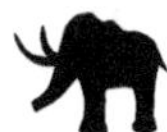

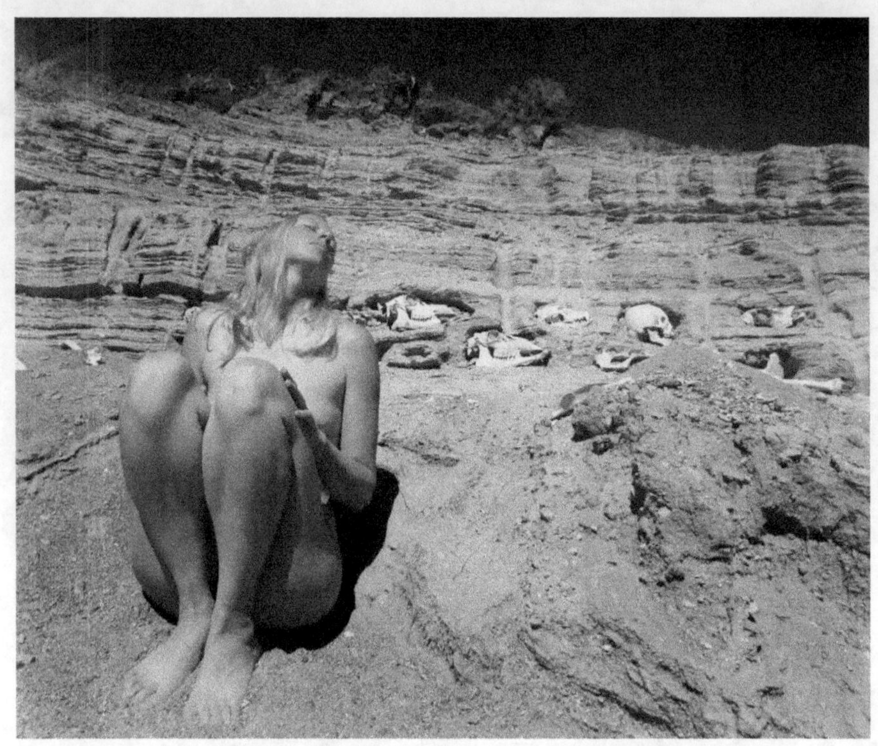

In the red dreaming light, mythic shadows
lean out from the west and wait for us
Movement is the nature of becoming.
Moving, these successions pass through the mind,
past migrations of memory since time out of mind.
The flight of birds witnessed at a point in its greatest rising
as the herd gallops away beyond the point.
Our movement northward, unpredictable in its continuing newness
straining toward an all-enveloping future.
Mithra's plains: movements from as far away
as the Kurdish hills, across the Oxus, with all the evidence of priest craft,
the slashed fetlocks and the moment having forgotten
that our bones were gathered, for the nonce,

along the way in a bull's hide.
Hordes of beasts and the men among them: across beds
of cracked patellas,
a god unknown by name passed here,
the washes and edges strewn with blanched phalanges
which point the way to the desert range submerged in stars.
Behold the lichens, fragrant in the muted color!
Boulders yet warm shift in their aroma.
The young volcano gurgles in its sleep.
How closely the universe presses against our backs!
Behold the Stella to forgotten gods.

The singular track lies before us.
Trees in full leaf, flowers in full bloom and all the horned
gods adorned with garlands!
Or, a great forest ridden down by ambling yellow tractors
dragging enormous iron anchor chains between them—
trees piled in ugly windrows.
The ancient tribes must endure without their piñon nuts,
as the mountains watch
as from a dream based on beautiful truth.

Was there always this sullen lull in meaning after the
passionate exhalation brings evening across ravaged earth?
Hordes and all cities overrun again by eternity.

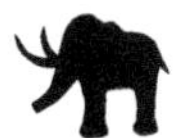

O you know me well enough, long enough
how I disagree adamantly with those
I forewarned for so long; reproachfully,
that look—a probing spine in a phrase, a hook,
which makes me feel caught upon a tongue
—their tablecloths, fatigue, pleasantries annoy
and now my luck: down to my last snaky skin,
canny radar scanning:
winter's gaze homing-in;
microwaves leaking-in.

Mark our flight desert-ward
as this dun bird sings on:
stay with me; the last frontier seen again
in second sight tastes of summer, black on white;
dark reverses night to light.

Beaches dry in alkali. Combing the beach
beyond the talus end, considering footprints
trailing back beyond shifting memory's end,
the old trails in dim city streets, now forgotten,
slip away to the sand.

And we talk, we walk the bottoms of vanished seas;
tongues buried in aquifers speak once more;
memories in murmuring waters move
in lost oceans' pounding centuries.
A shark's tooth, pick it up; another rumination.
Keep it up.

Astonished—startled vision—the crossing patterns—
these lozenge marks cannot be snakes, and yet some are.
Snakes gather squirming in our shadow-shapes,
crawl within the fated homunculi who follow our feet;
dual trails lost in sand, we cast our simian shapes asleep—
As we walk, we watch and we ourselves are watched as
slow motions moving in mirrored glints in lizard eyes
following us out among the old dunes.

Restless rocks, their vertical particulars,
their horizontal generalities,
profusions on the desert.
Pediments move away as far as our eyes can see;
saliences with similarities, oppositions,
attractions rise.
This is the plexus:
its black stones hunch, become recumbent
(where the Creature lies).

Feel the Creature's mood—a running time, ancestral
wind, a dying song the shaman sang—shaman, shaman
whose summer brown hands are gone; hands which shaped
these glyphs; astral stones touched in wonder,
we touch.

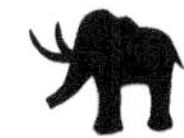

On my hands and knees—my search
for the evidence finds not a bone
Roaming lightning strikes the same juniper,
over and over again.
How did we come to these, our usual evil customs?

Mourning doves succumb with incurable sadness,
crowding the branches in contorted pines,
in recumbent junipers, where I too would lie,
joining lamentation.
Their sorrow too low for human ear to hear,
too soft, so sad that only the heart attends.

Yes, sorrow for silent birds;
sorrow for the sentient herds
the rains brought out of long eras of thunder
great territories, bouts and jousts,
the bloody horse and warm gregariousness.

Odors of rut and manure on lost plains
the upturned lip
tasting sensual air, the stallion sensing the mare
now vanished, trackless, without trace.
Peace to the flocks; peace to the herds;
The coyote tells me of something
born out of despair, a starving pup.
The truth has been forgotten.

I am exhausted with this long memory;
I have hacked too many ribs from spines,
have drunk black blood from skulls
of my infrequent sleep
in occluded dreams, charged with death.
Smiling gods informed me.
Ancient was the cauldron on its sooty tripod,
long were my conversations with the deities
formed en repoussé.

Once among remorseless waves and smoking stumps,
lightning struck, women, quiet, coietal, with their wolves.
I search for the one who once was here, as in a light night fever.
her belly swollen with secret hysteria and private laughter,
her taut stretch marks a moon-lit sky.
Her mother, her mother's mother the one who was here once,
the virgin who set a jewel in nostril
painted the spot between her eyes
with bright blood of her menses.
Then the cry in seizure, and coiled, with darting tongue,
the cool night, has disgorged its stolen eggs.

I haunt the plain searching for her, speaking out to wandering
winds warm breath; I stretch out on a white loam
and roll in my ancestors ashes before I return to the congress of men
filled with anger, doing all things poorly,
their speech the speech of idiots,
overheard at the half opened door, many mumbling of war.

The libation from the great mountain flowing from the
seasons at the forest threshold—
I pray this violent shore is its own undoing
Please speak of immolation; even here Har Oden is watching.
I taunt the being with many names relearned,
the dialect indistinguishable from my ancestors voice.

Facing seaward,
confronting the reckless world with unassigned directions,
the lank tulles wave
on my retina, pupils closing to pin pricks,
the slow motion moving downward.
This whole year was a loss of memory at high tide,
a too long poem, too intangible to finish.

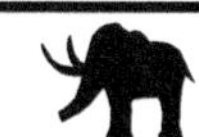

Our lives are not here, not these, the few penguins
left to shores of extinction, left to bleached whale bones
rusted escutions, broken fuselages.
We knew the mortar stone was a cavity ground by centuries
under other suns.
At the blazing estuaries, midday, the sky in mid-stride,
boulders were women bent at task.
They, the women who fed us pestled the lotus, the camas to whey,
deepened the cavity, the manos worn to knobs,
the patient meals.

Level is our sight at the vast stage;
now, distant shapes take form, a lingering audience after the act.
Watching the horizon for rising planets, between the acts and after.
The angus bull with heavy scrotum smells his cows from afar,
his position at the higher ground, our position in anger,
on all fours in scrutiny of the Sign.

And we are watched, they are watching;
the fracture is random and conchoidal.
Then, tremors palsy the hand, the side the stroke struck
at a time the austere moon rose to the occasion with
brighter stars.
Hiatus falls across the world and commuters stall on steel bridges
by a night threatening insanity with absolute clarity—
the most distant stars in numbers comprehended only by computers.

Huddled in lodge pole pine, we come upon agreeable quail
a dog hair thicket; malodorous weasels oil the night
with musk and deception.
—Fragments!

—Shivered from weathered surface, appalling features are revealed
in crazed stone spalled away and split at the strain
where rock contracted, cracked, stained with tears
for Niobe's slain children.

For the thousand years and the millennium after, it is
precisely here spring comes, showing in dawning motes
with black bees and prairie falcons hovering over the age,
the grey sage greening out with that panting fever
coyotes bring to the hills.

It is here; one more spring I would like to see with the
grand returning, birds in conjured clouds
I would like to see again from the eye-level of boyhood, once again.
I smell the smoke, the meals, millions ago.
Who were these women who fed us, giving birth to some
feeding their sons dreams of errant fires.

But in the fire of beckoning dreams the rim rocks now sadden
and where they end at the earth's edge profiles have become hatchet-
faced
and watchful. The source is poisoned; the tailings are perfidy
piled high and mendacity lies where the face has been blasted away.
Here the petroglyph is pock-marked, a target.
And the yellow road sign warns of the black snake
which curves ahead on a road no longer traveled,
            another road that failed
as language fails under this acid cloud which erodes my greatest dream.
The women wait at the edge of enormity.

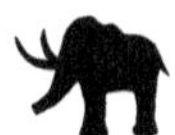

Sharp quills whistle,
reflect quick grey streaks from evening water
fading light, the mourning doves.

Look here, here these deep blue dreams
burst with orange light and something wants to be born;
something is in the inside, nudging.
But is there any use to tell you of the wind's velocity
and of the stubbornness of roots and rocks,
of the quickness of our passage in sight of these massive
watchful cliffs; is there any use?

Precious Gaia, again expectant,
what may we expect from your moon torn womb?
was our leash too long or somehow twisted?
Know that harlequin death in white face
has already learned our obscene dialect.
Oh yes, he knows the secret speech
of the epicene and self elected.
Oh precious mother
mother of pearl and tortured gold,
we bury your bairn in inlaid boxes.
But something wants to be born.

Have I told you how long I've been offended,
Moon, that burns my dreams!
Sun, that gives me life!

Walking through the decimation, dead mastodons,
minglers of prayers, the distant kin, eaters of foes.
Under the capstones dream infamous kings with their
murdered retinues, wild-eyed horses and strangled women,
laid out in obedient circles
in their fine gold harness and peculiar jewelry,
in holy earth, in immolation
in imitation of the endless heaven dome.

Here their marks are left as hands in silhouette
against the hard face, their marks, their hands,
pecked and tattooed through the desert varnish to the living rock
this image of the hand that held the stone
against the stone: hand that struck symbol: ram and bird.
Murderous thee creator who signed the stone
and piled the cairn.

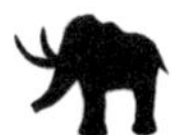

"And the beat goes on" – Sonny Bono

Sleet proof, we stood at the north in pleated shirts of seals' entrails,
Comfortable in the insides of others.
How in the busy centuries have we multiplied silences?
How between the undertow and periodic beaches we endangered,
supplied the license to overgrow, overthrow the species?
In a time of changing fortune, stung by insolence and embers...

The sinking fleets and flaming sheets, we sued for peace, too late,
As the ships went down, the shouts went up, west of Messana, at
Mylae, in special honor, sat the Roman boarding parties.
The cry, the cry.

Across the centuries, in their impossible ditches in the bullets spatter,
The white priests lay with the stain,
and the blowflies drowned with the clatter of helicopters.
My Lai, My Lai! We wash our blackened hands at the bleeding trenches
and sit down at last to a pleasant dinner with a sickening odor and listen
for the latest report of earthquakes in trembling California.

I choke on the admission that so many of our campaigns
        begin to sound alike.
Centuries, time, I shall initiate a lawful suit against you
        and your awful business
For yet a higher figure, too high to defray the expenses.
Oh, how?

Leave me with this taste of dirt in my mouth, for it was I
who slew the last mastodon...
And blame me for the carrion the magpies like.
The infallible vulture follows us out across the rift in time and expanses
where we died, inveigled the blind
to follow without us in a broad band
along the rifts and old migratory archipelagos.
But, as usual, it's probably too difficult
for you to understand what I'm talking about,
as far flung an abstraction as this one seems to be.

There was no water left on the whitened verges
for the Miocene flamingos,
faithful to their constellations.
Fateful, we walk hand in hand, too far out in the emaciations,
lost, caught between times like those geologic epics I've come to know.
Great movements in the ever watching sands reflect
the sound of the grey crane's distant whispers.

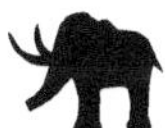

Ubi sunt?

Take note,
this age pounds past us at the gallop,
leaders running abreast
with human kind left to their own deadly devices,
left behind like funning monkeys
caught in nakedness
and their usual ignorance of everything,
gibbering over territories,
living hand to mouth,
recalling nothing of that brief time
when we ate the world's cattle
and grazed the world bare.

Rifts rest like beached, laden ships
waiting for the millennial tide;
they ride the sand, weathering,
filled with astonishment,   abandoned in bereavement
when time thinned and drained away all life.

Born to the task, the test,
never at a loss,
we, the best,
sowed seeds of greatest expectation;
a ragged landscape,
we find our own dried skins
in the pale winnowing.
Land of milk and honey, swans
and descending webs fall upon the day.

Layered schist holds secret its garnets
until the grand sky curdles one million times
and the dark red dyes, rolling in mica,
roll away their facets, sand, and mullet bones.

Age gains new title as amber eggs idle in eddies,
the tumid streams become white with milt
the color of milk in swelling spring.
And then the rain.
I smell my childhood
in the damp hour after the storm.

I have taken note of improbable creatures
in culverts and abandoned basements.
This creature lingering about in drunkenness,
or this one in trance state approachable,
but unrecognizable, without clear outline,
hanging, flapping in silhouette,
like a washing of clinging black sheets,
hung out, left out, after dark.

And so it goes
for a people born without memory,
born to easy tasks at the greatest harvests,
yet plagued by imagined dinosaurs
at odds with the unimaginable,
these great movers in dreams,
the fleeing things bleating
and hobbling away on their stumps
in the fresh cut swath.
What a harvest!

...cont.

...cont from pg 103

Next, what shall we do with our dissolute,
our lewd and lascivious, layered upon layers,
those governments within government
not even gods could invent;
And our women clad as bull baiters
who taste of chemicals,
their hair combed in phenol,
who swim with sharks
and take bestial thoughts to heart.
They couple with sinister mammals
in broad daylight, at home in day glow,
the holy women only their crotches veiled.
Their mates, bipedal, seeing to their needs,
crouching, swearing fealty to the Unnamable.

Where have gone all those musky girls?
They were seen as late as yesterday,
followed by their black dogs
freshly returning
from rolling on the dead
and newly bloomed lupine.
Women heading the weather,
nostrils flared,
who took account of birds' omens,
gathered at the late fires by the old lake,
traded powders and prattle
and mythological seeds.

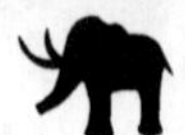

Where was my Mother
when mornings rang
the air with other wings?

She was seen standing at the city gate
consuming the morning star;
wrought in gold,
the city wall jeweled her hair;
or, there at the python's lair,
thrice I called her name, and she appeared,
her lions rampant and held at arm's length.

But I recall her best squatting by the river's
widest meander, her living tree at hand,
her finger pointing to the nest.

Oh, yes, I was her child, when
in the middle of the sea of stars.
All the dead swam back to life
and the whole realm was viewed again
and the eternal incarnate filed forth
to our rites of passage.

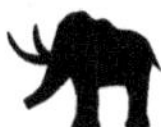

The nearly peaceful would pasture with all poets grazing
on one another's ponderous rhymes.
This is the way after the dark wind, grit upon the floor
and the taste of darkness upon the tongue.
And for the seeds that lie, the storm meant water for the drought
and the evening's dark powder is laid where the wind has lain
and the roots make room for the dead.
The arbutus blossoms for the bees as it does for everyone
blooms for the dead like strawberries bloom.
Flowers cured the lesions where the legions walked.
Upon the old mountain wrinkled in wisdom
green pasture and this year of the grebes
with their melodic questions, querulous melodies.
Young river from the old mountain, and no sign of man.
Young river at the bend casts a lazy smile across the land
and at the signal from the prompter
all waterfowl rise with the flowers in standing ovation,
in celebration.
A sacred session forms to the altar by vestal virgins.
In the morning before the heat,
young men brought before Apollo's temple
cast their urgent testicles upon the blood-stained marble.
I remember those unusual yellow evenings
alight with airborne spores
of immaculate orchids which mate
in sexual mimicry with the jungle wasps.

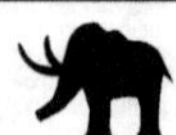

The preacher voids love,
shrills his message of briar thorns against a blank sky.
The way the slag is piled,
again a terrible face is formed in appalling quietude
except when a hard wind blows
but even then it's still horrific.
Anyone can see that hatred
was the main occupation here.
Any other work was covered over
by what was left of those sad hours
which are in no way redeemable
even by the best memory.
Only an ancient Iranian goddess
could make something of benefit
from the ashen garden.
Where is sublime Amosa Surya Anahita
when everyone of any good sense
cries out for boon in a garden called Eden?

Who could have imagined that this land
would have been strewn
with uncountable elephant skulls
in such a little eye-blink of eternity?
Memory fills with flowers
and like old flowers fades.
Each generation carries its memories
with little say, nothing more.
Even as we speak,
slag accumulates under every footfall,
as dust devils mix in
with the preacher's hateful drone.

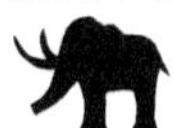

Centuries flutter and beat upon our dying faces.
Our idols are buried or sunken in the mouth of a red sea
revealing pearls as atolls in waves of language
or are they departed Greeks at high tide
sailing the red wine sea at rosy fingered dawn?
No, it's the day's brains bashed out against the sky,
crimson fringed, changed at black night
finally to stars of consciousness.

Dawn prods the numbness with fatal stares and red swords
and numerous words rising on morning wings,
and yet the cycle sings in resurgence.
Even the high tree line has become a nesting place.
In valleys heat grows the molds of existence, our very fungus
is the warbler's insistence among the bull rushes,
but I know our gorgeous cougar is pacing the empty hills in vain.

The leaves' decay makes an arresting smell,
the inexorable whirlpools suggesting my childhood fear of the vortex
and the large snakes which live under the black banks—
stay away, stay away.

Stand on the narrow strand with skeletal fish facing upstream
which point the way to the miraculous source, the cave.
The oracular goddess issues council never more sought
in this age when the stop gap measures the last gasp.
Move over, prime mover, dust is descending.

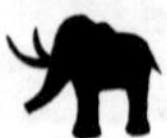

Our Wide Margins

Book 3

Love & Relationships

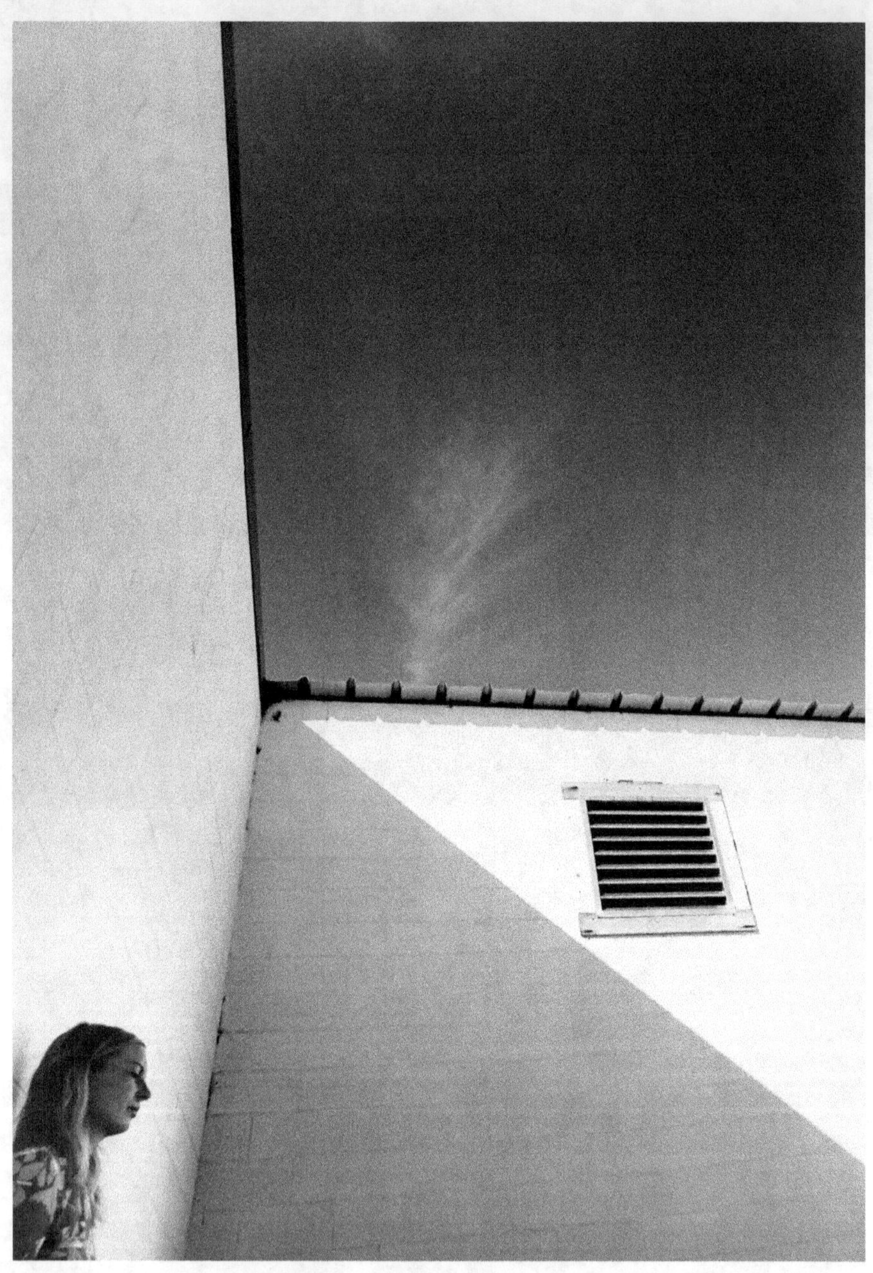

Almost Unnoticed

The tearful ground vent forth a wind of crimson light
that conquered each sense and like one
gripped in sleep, I fell.
Inferno III

That cloud is the word in the panchromatic sky:
the silver ghost giving up
a feather weighted against a feather, a silent cirrus
almost unnoticed:
a sheer sigh in the spinning sky, that exhales
from deep split soil as a final rattle
from the precious land.

Tar tears weeping, multi-lanes winding over
America, end in rutted roads to nowhere;
All over America the ghost is giving up with a sound
like a rattle from bones and ashen songs.
Lost songs remembered in a dream, found floating
in the dream-stream
flowing back through the years and beyond the steady
beat of native geese, nearly gone:
swans of childhood sung of spring migrations
on etesian winds and those summer songs sung
through summer leaves which wrinkled once and fell
frozen in the eternal stream flooding out

...cont.

...cont from pg 111

upon suffering ground
seasons flying, with time of no direction
the voices singing in the future from the past
singing only to me in dreams.
Gone is the song. The ghost is giving up!
And we remain for a time in this
fleeting space and hold:
in surrender to the solar force that breaks the
prison wall in luminous moments in fugitive flight.

Fugitive amid the ruins, surprise amid the ruins, these
linear vertices, edging velocities—
verities running out, lost
beyond the senses
in transitory flight in horizons past Orion,
seen deep beyond the ravens eye in a battlement of stars.
The total minute in its precious singularity
passed almost unnoticed
before we died.

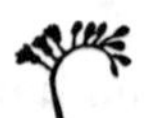

And there you are, uncovered,
showing me your back
rising and falling
dreaming about your inane longing
for some place where I am not.

And when you awake, I know all your love
was spent in that place of insane songs
and crowded bodies,
and that you will no longer love me.

Light cuts through the morning ink
and makes its sharp distinctions.
You will awaken soon, blinking,
damning the relentless light,
light which will cover your restless dream
and discover your lies.

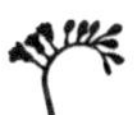

Can you recall my hesitation,
my knock at your door?
You invited me in to a roof caved in,
piled deep debris.
We stood in the four corners,
little room to sit or lie,
no talk at all of the serious conditions
revisions, decisions.

I carefully followed your circuitous
thoughts through the worming incisions
silverfish left in wallpaper flowers.
And then in faking lateness,
you crept away somewhere,
left the sifting wreckage to me and the
open ceiling, confusion of disaster.

I lay back in plaster, lath and splintered glass
looking up at black night sky, the sidereal sway,
the alarming speed.
The shivered stars left streaks,
and I wanted to tell you
how a cloud streamed fleet
over your dream, nocturnal pale body.

Speaking to the straining walls
I could not tell you they seethed and fluttered,
how poplars muttered and dogs barked
the dark wind. I wanted to tell you,

but a deep sound overcame me,
and I let myself out, groped beyond
the dead traffic light
and found an empty freeway.

How we become more despite the wreckage.
Now, headless of the weathering and something else
I wanted you to know before I left, I forgot.
I have returned to your door several times
only to find it fallen in
and a tall pine forest
growing in your driveway.

Do you recall my visit?

Confession of a shape shifter

The time has come to show you our territory I've laid out
between the freeway and the logging grade,
but the moon makes my eyes run, my neck swell.
Black flies pester me and you have vanished again.
There is little left other than the usual snorting
and to polish my horns against the slash.

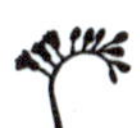

Autumn light that blushes in sight of me,
This heavy love that squirms and casts about inside
is like a troubled fetus long overdue.
Help me bear my love.
I am drowning in the centuries.
In this world of countless daughters, I am drawn only to you
I have waited long at the aerie where
Death shrouds all under one wing.
I have stood under the world tree to hear gnawing at the roots;
I move restless under surging red skies with
blood pounding seconds in my ears.
How many seconds?

These thousand fluttering creatures who watch over me as I sleep,
Sibyls in my dreams, serene beings each with the same benign word,
tender voiced mothers, damn mouthed and oracular goddesses,
wide eyed...
Your gentle hands warm me, guide me in my passage,
your white arms hold me through the blackest night.
Even now in your not too distant whispers
I hear the early geese, their sibilant quills and morning murmurs.

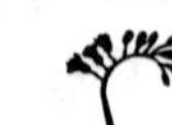

For Marian

Between bodies lie
        Great distant and vast coldness
                Sights and sites of pines
Dormant as slow resin
        Where patient mule deer stand
                Starving under the impassive junipers.
The sage is dry and odorless
        The Manzanita, brittle, surviving.
                All waters have hardened in
The terror grin of the owls voice.
        Muffled shadows of silent feathers
                Sweep over ground luring out
The nodding mice from underground.
        Hungry deer gnaw the bark
                At lower branches, stand up
Browsing higher, then pull down
        A sudden hoary shower.
                Frost glints everywhere.
Cricket calls trapped in
        Crystals fall silently in this frozen air
                In this far distance between us.

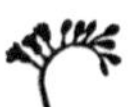

For some reason, or unreason, I appreciate you.
Is there really something going on between us
or is it only the wind shifting everything
around to suit itself—the errata drifting toward
the corners and all around failing light, the deception
in lengthening shadows as my stride quickens?
I hear you, and I'm looking everywhere, listening,
or is it the risen moon laughing over the lake?
But there you are again, your tragic face erased in
reflections all too bright.

More than twice a day I would take your measure
then my cool springs quench your brain
in my valleys
now the fountains yet flow
my oceans filled with every wonder, every pleasure.
Now in my days
of endless nights,
my storming tides have brought from
my deep dwelling its monster,
its mouth filled with endless rows
of razors
beached and hopeless not helpless.
Sirens rising, the eye glint of menace.

Once you told me that only the hounds of death
could part us and now death is at hand
star-crossed love.
A bird shrilled for one moment
omen in extremis.

Generations and days reciprocate
like fast cylinders, hot bearings in corrosive oil.
The long script of ambiguous weather
tells us something of what's to come
in the rash at dawn, the wrath at sunset
as the day's event is counted in corpses
and night shrugs its shoulders.

Under platinum stars as hours slide
on bearings of hard nipples definitely in the intimate,
very small ships with chromosomes in full court
come aground immured in uterine walls
helmets, horses and boarding parties.
The future is here in spite of the
dragons and the benzene.

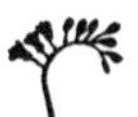

How glad I am you're here:
stars are looking, stones watching.

The morning sun is all: with morning sun
we are again.

I come to record our whispers
to decipher the sighs between the audible and inaudible
between spasm and sleep. Feeling-flash and thought-catch
on revelation: that sudden turning, suddenly
the eagle is more golden in the sun.
I follow its floating wings beyond waving boughs
deep cerulean chunks show through amorphous trees
and the eagle steers hard against the gust,
falls back, vanishes past the bluff.
A driven rain, leaves raining,
aspen leaves bury my face with Baudelaire and his
memories of a thousand years; his face emerges
from the ruins—homage á Baudelaire—
attended by Señor Dali's nuns, wimples
like chrysanthemums growing in the tumbled columns
and it seems, I am bedded with Nietzsche's woman
by whom I will never have children, "Ich liebe dich, oh Evykeit..."
Such promise in day's voices beginning: dawned red
wings outspread, long files fly southward.

Love is in beginnings, blessing wind touches faces,
blessing hands and flocks head in, mount upward,
sight the sun's emergence before first rays
strike across the land.

The magpie calls, beckons at the edging hour,
knows that time rubs our flesh,
rubs our lines
our faces, but the old palimpsest still may be read
through all argument and erasures,
I remember you....

Dream long between the sips of swirls
in your yellow hair.
a sun that I know is yellow, of a life that I know is bright
She seeks with heat the warm prey.
She makes the American scene dressed to kill
as some say.
The viper rests in brown flesh with rattles hid
lies in wait.
You must remember that a snake once teased
may bite itself to death.

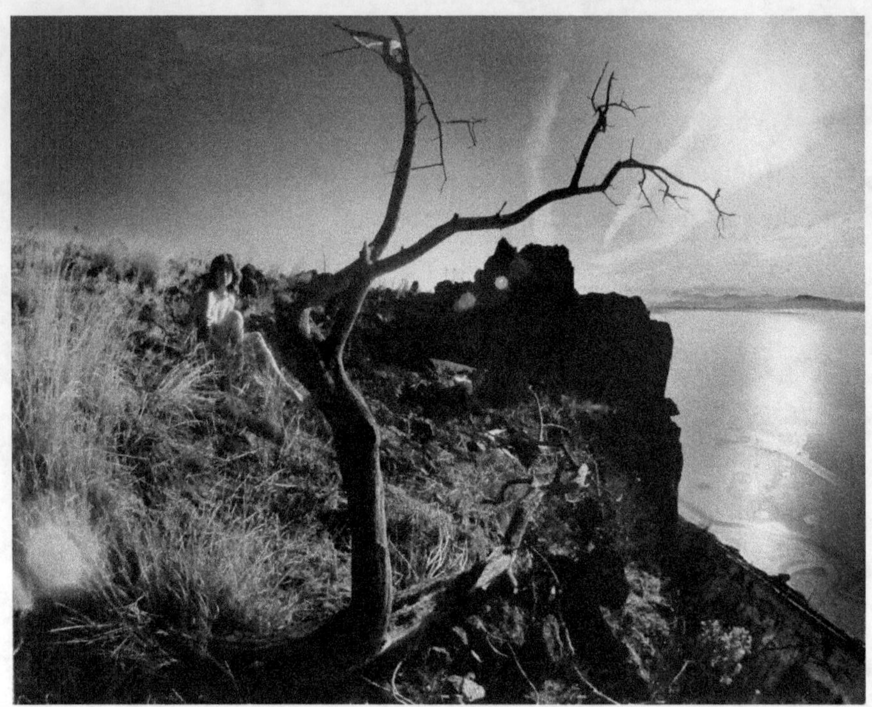

Human skin under the cold sun
Tanya in the nude on the winter mountain with
time all around and running out.
We are pregnant with beaming children and bright ideas
but the hard sun bears and burns necessities and the snag trees,
limbs bare, turn pointing fingers.
Stones are leg-long shadows
that flee to the open arms of the somber horizon
the last flood, sun, earth, with all its burdens settles.
The great night is voiceless.
All stars are hidden from the cities

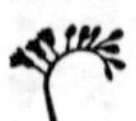

I am not yet finished with the story
because the story is not yet finished with us.
Sending forth a scribe
gulls mew, ravens croak.
A body welkin wants royal birth.
All crania stare and become powder
when touched.

In this latest drama all the
props are in place: behind them is eternity.
Beside them
are the actors scandal and excuse.
Ethereal purple deepens.
The audience is real, people black-filled with stars
that wink as if showing a lake which almost comprehends.
An ambulance rushes and with it another
day loaded with emergencies.
The I lumber brought you is peppered with knots.
I'm not certain that you'll ever speak to me again.

I see the moon after night land coasting
in the morning with the other smaller
shapes, retinal forms I could only hope
to see, wish to see beside the pelvic
cups and the mons in morning breeze steady.
But look! The magpie still lands all over
the oak, a caustic flirt, in the middle
of the bright, light wind, critiques all progress
in untranslatable language cut through
with opportunities of persisting.
Black flies, sweat drunk, sated in ecstasy:
all encouraged by the gaining blue sky
containing nothing but the sun to hold
the dreams before the dying which isn't
so damned sweet, not pleasure. Motion in the
amnion turning on the umbilical:
watch for plural catching, aortic arch
bursting, inherited in first moments
of the ova and sperm. Poor slow cervix moves,
dumb and blind, in the wet morning perfume,
drinks at the semen pool and bleeding fresh
from the neck, caught by the cat, in the jaws
of the genetic cat, half snake, half cat:
waxes and swells luten-shaped like the moon.

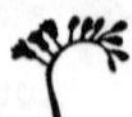

In Absence of Marian

In dark forest's perfect still
owls tell me of the cold.

speak to me, dear Marian,
of how and where and
what you are so we
both may know.

Speak in your native thoughts
of cranes in concert which rise
and wheel from the Oregon plain,
of the age before mankind when all
was sharp color and matchless time,

of your heart's desire
of your will to know
of you
of me

with your warm breath which
chills the pain.

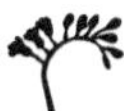

I've been looking for you.
I have another lament to give you.
So smothering is this drying white skin
covering the planet.

I've been looking into poisoned wells of green water,
through dangerous towers of air from any position
the body assumes in the course of dreaming.
I am servant of the dreams, the flight always
above, the fright below and looking outward
brooding volcanoes: those are the cries of children,
and more and more children.
Burning, destined for ashes, noise as terrifying as
rotting wood or the black spoor pour which from the
withered bag.

Listen.

Here is the dark room filled with kisses and this large
bouquet of blood.
Here a patient building rots in rain; the river fills with
shredded red wings; gorgeous mountains which
remember everything slump with time.

And you, when I touch you, oh when I touch you,
you shake like the fragrant withers of a horse.
When last I explored your body for its seasons and
memories, I searched your eyes for the moon set over
nacreous beaches of white semen; between your legs
was the soaked hair of a floating
man found drowned.

Always I was looking for you; I am the one you saw
on the exploding shore, the ground up bones; here caught

gazing into the privacy of the spider's geometry;
at my temples, my throbbing petioles.

I am the one you left, a door left ajar
amid pain and long winter remembering single white clouds
rising importantly as petitions against a dying sun
clouds as beautiful as the marble eyes which yet look seaward
from the Erechtheum.

In this fictitious desert you may hear the brine crack
at high noon as nuptial rats in secret whistling and chattering
in total darkness.
I should receive applause and a disinterested ribbon
then shot with traitors.
Over there and alarming are the metal tubes filled with death
odors more powerful than all the rotting bodies of dinosaurs,
tubes disguised and nameless guarded over by those who believe
in purple anthems.

Yes, I am telling you the truth. I can't promise you much.
If you may find your way back, I'll show you the
furious metals parked in bunkers. Come back, turn right where
the objection forks, where the bleeding god has given us nothing
more than this large box filled with human teeth.

Know that
something's changed, something's wrong
with the sea, something's wrong with me.
Oh, lucid birds, never could I speak and bring forth the arcane ursprache
We have altered creation, creation has faltered.
Destruction is here amidst us waiting to happen.
But yes, come back; we are yet alive
yet living in oblivion.

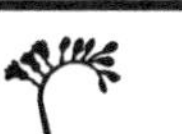

Once in tangled valleys,
this earth was strewn with so many places to love
with dappled sunlight, sun spotted birds.
Now caged mammals, damn,
we have chosen the doors of darkness,
old men with vacant looks in ageless alleys.
I muse here,
nurse the knuckles of the grudge in a garden
trellised by violent hours.
Bones begin to creak within me.
Where I strive to enter the morning, the sky is unscarred and uncaring.
Last evening was a dark passage of memory.
Now, the suddenness of sunlight and a single cloud, the juniper yet
smoking, split once more by lightning, and fevers rush past from all points.
Don't mock me.
All your shadows outcast, your footsteps overturned by emerging insects.
Your hours are impaled as the quarter moon assumes its amber mast.
To think that you cast your lot with the dead out of fear of the living,
because you fear the living,
and because I know the secret
floating in the lotus, I plot with the dead.
This universe has always been.
I sing to the angel who guards my bed.
The oracle's green eyes spasm in oblivion.
Your dark circles are eyes of orgasm.
Everywhere god is black in hornblende

and smiles benignly with the bronze idols seated
in their uncountable niches.
These are primitive times.
Now look at that ugly stone,
rescued from my oblivion.
What do you think now?

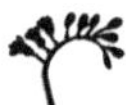

The day was filled with nails
and the blunt hammer. Finished day
punctured with sharp reports,
the river lost its geese.
Clouds under the sky
strange striae account for themselves.
Now behind the
blue mountains,
mountain time and river time,
time of the sky in this
transient place high piled with stones.

Yet this was for us to live upon
this planet with its
magnificent dead:
great joy of the throbbing rose
or this persistent passion for the truth
in canyons of cascading echoes.
Now this deadly unremitting rain
which always happens on overturned planets,
those laments poured
into the flowers' hungry mouths.

Here the future has happened
and over there again: the burning acrid plastic
in the corridor, our whore with her skin on fire
and that awful weeping from within the walls.

Farewell, farewell, a spiral stairwell
of abandoned conversation.

Now a very wide street filled suddenly
with velocity and momentary eyes.
Must I sleep in your doorway assailed by shadows,
pierced by syllables?
I am at a loss for sound,
for words describing this oceanic feeling
of being here with you,
our thoughts turned upward
to this fast running sky of white scars.

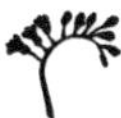

Sometimes I doze sitting upright
like one of my brooding rifles in the rack.
This morning I wanted to tell you about my guts
but I refuse to dose myself
with sentimentality.
The bathroom mirror caught me.
I drew close and stood for a long time.
My eyes welled. I rushed away to bury my head
under a sick motorcycle.

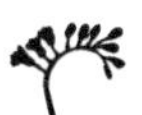

The moody rain without,
he grumbles about the chaos within his head
and the noise of his voice paints the year
gray with fog, and misfortune.
Weary rain,
mushrooms, cervix-like, dilate
within in the flesh which
is nothing at all when promised
altars strewn with yellow garlands
nothing when
the fallen vaults have covered the echoes
and in spite of the pelvis's perfect curve, our hours have
devoured the land,
a reason why I have come to know so well these dead rivers
filled with antique rock in the wake of centuries.
Oh, my father, in search of signs of the guilty ones.
Oh, my sister, with whom shall we live now?
We seek the deep distant green, the horse tail ferns which rise
in ancient brotherhood with their attendant fronds of silence.
Here my father stood in search of signs of the guilty
in lacquered lateness, last lights from the far decimations
in a shower of glittering lance heads upon a
high range of amnesia.
Mascara makes your eyes awesome flowers with black stamens
in an evening scape blurred with tears
the bending heliotrope
your mouth turns down as red flowers in evening sky.

Tomorrow's weather: white hives and golden swarms

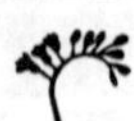

Yellow salve and funerial gauze changed daily
two broken legs, skins of withered shins
in a lifetime never healed.
Goddamn.

Two osteomyelitis in rotten marrow began
I recall my uncle groomed
only in his windings.
Goddamn.

Seated on the lawn alone with a soft-on
since his youth, longing and swearing
caught in the sag of his used-up skin.
Goddamn.

Brain blood erred, sapped speech from his head
but glinting and muttering on his bed
until the end, he cried.
Goddamn, goddamn.

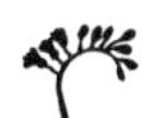

Since wandering here before,
Often I come back,
Come back to ask what happened,
Since wondering here before.
Walking now with you,
I come back to break the silence,
To speak of this with you:
This whole day made of faultless American sky
And this often thing I should report,
Empty roads into empty dead ends,
Past stairways to nowhere,
By gutters and drains.
Yes, you remember, you were there,
the track of our lives in colossal piles,
cold cream jars and spent pressure cans.

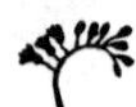

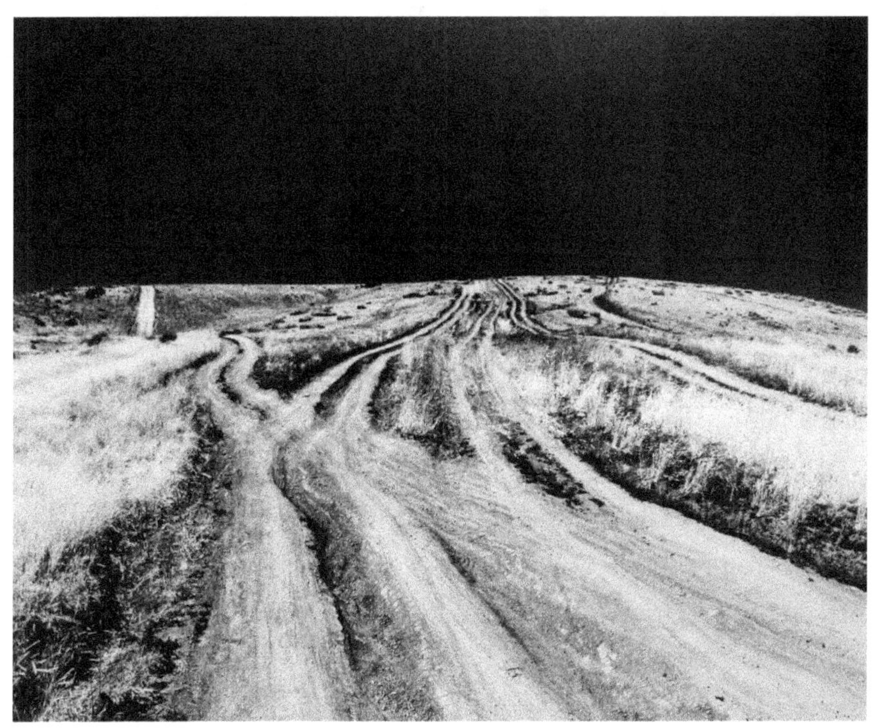

"Les Routes a Nulle Part"

Valarie Becomes a Butterfly

And then we heard it coming, a great black beast alone
deaf to its own drumming—fumes of diesel and ozone
a locomotive heard as in a dream pursued by the unforgettable
sky lowering its curtains in black pulsations
and a half-earthly lowing from somewhere.

Beauty your breast is fluttering—beauty your beast is throbbing
past an overpass across the tunnel to eternity
echoes sobbing from the underpass
night hawks soaring, roaring
that other day the beast was that sweating angus
rank among us, beast with bloody brow
goring his own unprotected flank until the very last gasp
and mourning swans sang with church bells, farewell.

Girl, grasp the compact action
man dressed in unforgiving flesh is an angry animal,
very dangerous to himself, very dangerous indeed until
the last gurgle.

no ifs ands or buts, this air was ruined in a thrice
for we were never told in a crisis a trial balloon contained
a somber bomb,
beauty, beauty at least we are excused from further duty
Your fair share at the wind's edge?

At the sandy funnel
the ant lion inters the ant at the angle of repose.
Hope becomes dust and lies in vastness.
Dung blows through windy streets past us.
No pain in winding sheets however wound, no return
not with this mizzling wind which awakens the most
obstinate seeds in dithyrambic spring.
Seasonal lamentations, wet clouds and logic of thunder
because of what conspires in the thunder under the skyline.
Light, distant flashing and something deadly in the rain.
What dire things confound us forming in miasmas, rising behind us.
In the age of ague and mud, chant of the tired, the many milling
a cry going up from the crowds
A return to augury and argument of divination.

Beauty, never blame the magpie for its prattle or the rattle
of poets or for that matter, god for changing tragic sisters
into magpies.
God's magic is transmutation
mindless twaddle is nature to magpies, as insanity
among the many heads of state, or pigs all comfortably a grunt,
supine in their pismire.

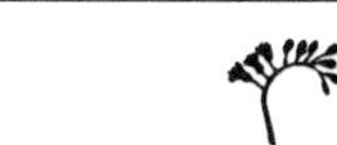

Walking barefoot in tall grass
my thoughts greening out
with nothing more important
than prying barehanded
the tails from scorpions
avoiding the sting
a risky meal.

Or how would it feel
looking out from under a beetled brow
my prognathous jaw set upon knuckles
while seated on my ripe ischial callosities
as the first thinker
considering scorpions in a more important way.

I keep trying to get a fix on it:
the pole star or why a crabbing wrinkle crawls
across your forehead's ticking brow,
vanishes with pressure from my cool thumb,
leaves a pleasant stigmata
a small full healing moon
on the mind flesh.

Thoughts still running astray
but soothed, quieting.
Why do I feel that angry growl
running my tender ribs
as the pleasant finger
slips under the mons in the family grip
as a special hunt?

I see a vicious snarl—teeth snapping,
hot saliva down a panic burrow—
the squirrel with a shorter tail.
And I feel the cruel bit pulling blood
from a tortured lip as I tongue the areola
then watch the bullet go to sleep
and fall unerringly to the gash that flows.
The shot punctuates soft munching:
an ungulate gumming-off grass with toothless uppers—
a deer falling down slowly,
slowly a deer fallen down.

I just can't focus on it anymore;
eyes refuse to hold it long.
I count on nothing but change and chance
this chance storm: the lightening
a billion volt
a master stroke against the blackest sky.
That instant espalier as it grows,
blinds the eye, knots my hands,
knuckles white, body stiff.
Lightning fell.
Seth bit his own tail
and he rolled, is rolling now,
eternized, swelling larger
twisting one coil upon the other
as the unending Mobius strip
laughing,
laughing like hell.

Your smile, wear nothing other than,
wear very well your own
contented animal:
widening femoral grin,
temporal feminine humor,
your femurs draw me in—
I die the death of those who
went before and of those who follow,
fathers fathering.

Stalled in the corners,
collected beyond the sunlight
so quickly the sun moved the shadows
across the wall— hour
after hour, shadows
lulling the hours.

I— your monkey
in dreams—hanging in your hair,
feed at your ears.
Tell me again how the garden pushed up
so fast, fell over.

Exploring his chasm bark,
the brown creeper scolds our hulking flesh,
and the ponderosas overshadow us, their
girth and great height
comfort and protect us.
Tell me again
how from such a small hair-lined nest,
how such big jays,
how such a rambunctious family, rasping,

flew straight away with their own
very blue, very own summer.
Tell me again...

Our garden conversation fills
with sentimental elements:
but, at night our sound is elemental
and of the ocean.

Wide between the eyes,
gat-toothed between the grin,
beautiful and all together loveable,
you may tell me again,
how between deep soundings
in the perfect water,
the grebes bugle the evening on.

We are a race washed up.
Was it here the waves washed us up,
left us gasping on the shore?
Or was it the wind that you might recall those flagella;
A waving anthology in the visceral night,
as your own sea flowers search for the ova.
In this cool hole worn by the vanished ocean,
My exploring finger traces in the stone, the inner shape of a woman.
My love has features like islands and oceans, chasms and wells.

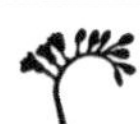

The Words Have Lied

Why doesn't my poetry speak
of the long last-blooming begonia
waiting patiently behind my bedroom window
reaching up with flowers as
pink as my fingernails
or a dragonfly's compound eyes
architecture grander
than a great cathedral,
hungrier than a fox.

It isn't useful, music isn't,
when all the words have lied.
We decide upon the methods of suicide
colliding enormity and extremity.
I am guarding the roads to oblivion:
I am neither here nor there,
you are here and there.
You insist on the ruined silence.
I have passed this way where so many things have come to pass.
Again you have ravaged the territory then denied the healing rain.

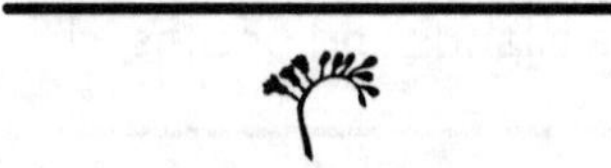

What can we say
when the sun takes us,
when the moon makes us
weep with longing
before that final lofty
glide into the vast invisible?

The day grows late in memory.
Remember the past,
gaze so far that you were a small
creature in a memory-scape of huge lizards
and deafening noise
and oceans choked with grass, and the instant
becomes the future. The soldiers there,
rising to face their long night,
make ready their brilliant bullets.
Then far far in time the armies tarnish
the mirrors fail
falls the moon and all the metals
with not one ibis on whose wings
I might write a message to my love.

Wallows and Washes

Book 4

Modern World & Politics

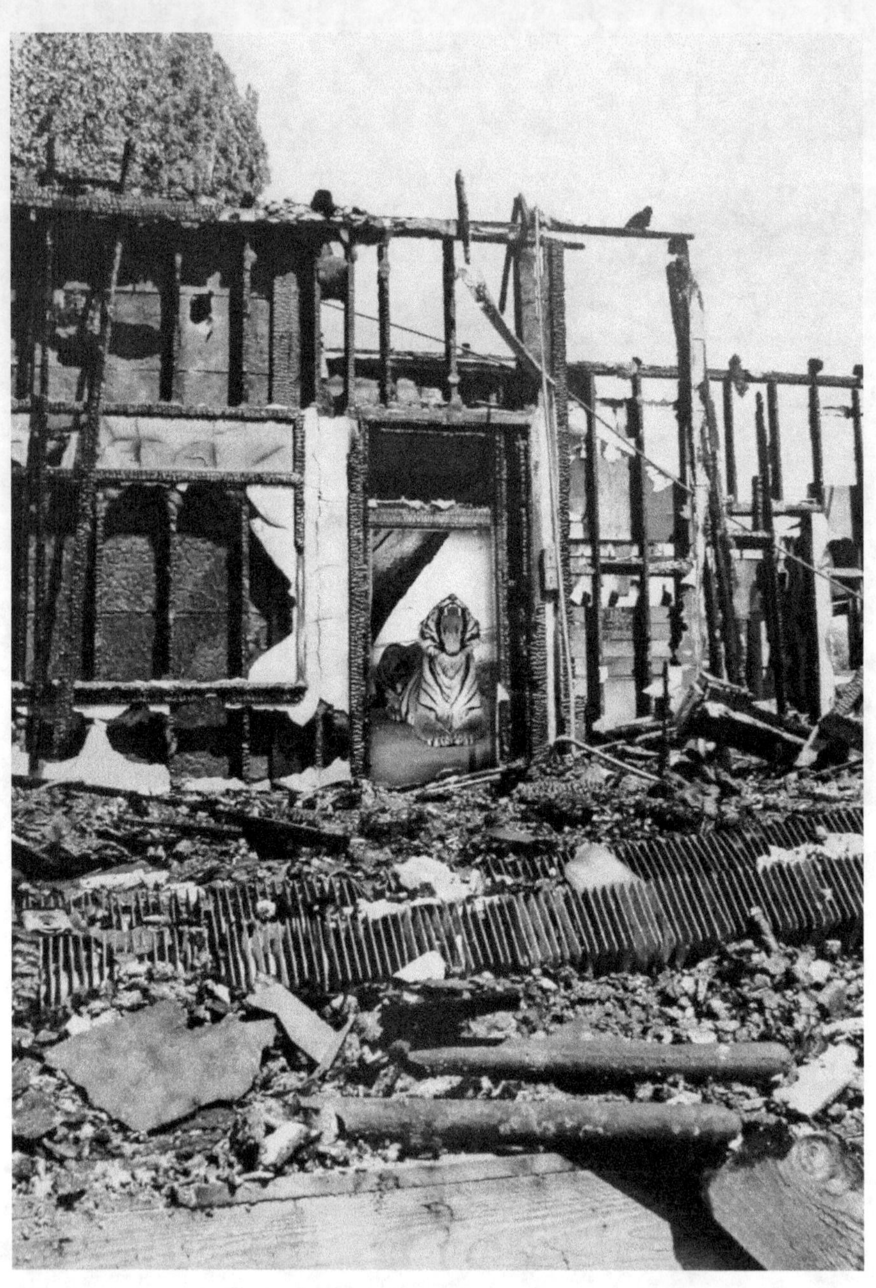

"Den Tiger ist Gleich"

-Nietzsche

We huddle close to our hearth stone, centering
the coals, tending the center, not afraid but
cold and out of sun; sleep, sleep.
The world has waited a long time for our
renouncement, the denouement, and the animals
have joined us, end with us as the dinosaur ended.
I can read the black glyph between the tiger's eyes,
this wild thing, stays with us until the end.
I wish for the dark ages, so called unfettered ages,
Bright light, unbound hope;
I would gladly take my chances with the plague.
I do anyway.
Well, let it pass.
I'm pissing on a stone, I know,
with my eyes on stars.

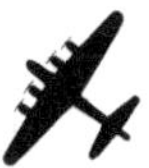

Rocks wade out, grand isles rise with the sun
and with the rising returns our far wandering shadow mimes
who must act out the new ape-ish elongations
learned during the night's dream.
All desert is theater, the audience is quiet stone.
The light indelible, the stage enduring dust.

I have returned to the red desert
to find my arch enemy,
but that was centuries ago.
I have come to this footpath
surrounded by the black and jagged buttes
overflown by the same old vultures,
but that was centuries ago.

Glory was never here. I'm not looking.
Virtue, if you seek it, is the bitter brush
that prepares itself when no one's looking,
then blooms yellow and suddenly
when everything else is dry and autumnal.

Low is the fierce killer, the desert eagle,
whose brown eyes fill with his own stunning horror
and great longing for his beautiful white eyases.
Primal bird, the same world without virtue,
but the mob is nowhere to be seen,

yet you may know by all that's missing,
that they have mobbed the scene.

Take a good look at the future
that's flung all around
in boulders and sky.
Note the footfall or what's pulled up or torn down,
all to make a nation.
Hell is the future
and, when the mob discovers itself,
will run like the devil.
All slave to find a master,
and anyone who can flatten a great forest
is again presidential timber.

The earth rolls, the stars ride,
and that mountain I know so very well
is the fountainhead of blackness.
The wellspring at the talus
is as polluted as any outfall from the septic city.
The ruin we dread is this ruin we tread.
Soon the sun will rise with so much work to finish,
our sun, potent, serene,
to which we may add or take away
nothing.

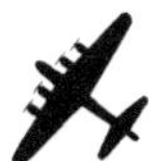

Another tectonic anomaly, plates lifting
or plunging under, lunging on the sleepers back
from savage light
deep in chthonic night at ritual temperature,
while the tribes of gods and gods of tribes
observe highest mass at the millennial altar.
As the new age signals its fumaroles
and guns of eternity, not cosmic with meteors flash,
but halide crash upon the seismic fact
that occupies the mind of a great terrestrial thought:
which is exactly what the hell is going on?
Crimes against humanity but no criminals
in the ongoing enterprise.
Is this a state of anomie?
If you want a pretty lily, just ask for it
but that god over there
lies mute in his casket.

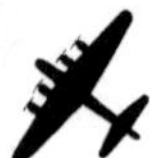

Beneath endeavor, forever, what we bequeath
the cyclopean night rears up one-eyed
but an earth described by speech is no description of our ways,
the manner of a dying shaman tending dyed plumes
set along abandoned trails.

Sleep is a myth revisited in the dilations of spring,
a spring seen again beyond the black accumulation
in man's visions, gathering above the horizon or beyond
where the ponderous lowing in the dust is heard,
the panting.

Are clouds the ghosts of dinosaurs lumbering
or teams in harness foaming red at cruel bits?
Are clots at sunset women's labor, the bitten lips?
The startled partridge flies to expectant rocks and
we hear shots reported in distortion from the reaches
in the far isolations. Here the gosling mistakes
the ewe for its parent and dies in confusion.

Here I learned
without revulsion to eat Christ's body.
All doors are open and the roads eventually
bring us to the Reactor,
to the leaking ambience, the iodine, the radon.
The symbols on the signs are clearly read
at the road to nowhere,
and dangerous is the work.
We reel now with the effects of the big swig.

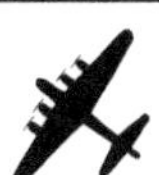

Aztecs! Again the time is come for religion
when priests wear the too-tight skins
of their flayed daughters, to praise the Lord
and stink of rolling dogs.
Can you imagine how Cortés was sore amazed?

The air, the ground, culprits all around:
A secret government,
false gods leave a wake of pitfalls;
With antique smile, Pandora steps forth
as the regime prepares further violence to mutilated air.
These homeless are hideous and oddly obedient.
The lonely lost crisscross the killing ground
in search of their true natures.

The reviled overturn the earth
in search of artifacts.
The guiled surprised
are photographed from afar, by those
disguised as true gods
but who fight among themselves
eavesdropping and
leaking secrets.
The regime worries.

Each day new words emerge;
but I'm not here to teach you new words,
you crypto-fascists,
narco-militarists.

Hwæt, Beowulf?
Hey there, dragons in smoke filled rooms;
I mean you,
new leaders, old serpents who slide
through the endless pentagonal corridor:
the abysmal odor that lingers in tombs
now malingers in towns.

Because I have touched these stones,
I have touched your life.
It's as if we were watching sunsets
on a planet not at all of our ken and
all laws mere anomaly.
As if those mountains were in the way
and all trees the enemy.
As if elephants and dolphins
were dealt with by death.
Our children fatherless, were futureless, and
with the plight of knowing it.
This is the hiatus in memory of life without
history, ditches and borrow pits along the roads
lead again to nowhere,
where city sepsis ends up somewhere,
where the speeches play out.
All the while
deft nets pay out by the mile.

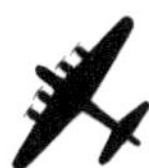

Be easy;
let down your hair;
the moment is coming;
we must succumb.

We were having tea on the balcony overlooking
while our glasses filled with ashes; yet
we have discussed the meaning of the word at length
and with ramifications.
Do we terrify the starlings
cowering in the eaves and drain spouts?
Even the rats have fled the city
leaving the city to the insane
a fatal terror in their popped eyes
their little pink noses
squealing in the smoke.
And look above!
Hunched gargoyles sing with chorus sores
weep the yellow stuff pain is made of.
Grinding from the rose window the cathedral sings
its rose a death wheel, rolls.
A baroque fumato thickens the fugue:
the droning organ
the great cicada
its wings spread to the clerestory.
Smoking specters hover over pleasure-pain
peel the long loops of elastic skin.

Distance and time
the long droning
with irksome soft arpeggios and evocative redolence
and in interstices pilloried heads and hands
and nuns suffocating
unceasing in their work struggle at the walls.

Be happy in your work immolated with the dolls
the kicking bundle wrapped is rolled between the aisles.
Gropes between the depilatoried legs of screaming school girls
boys asking randy priests for confession.

Distance and time...
the lawn pales; skin exfoliates; bells peal
chitinous claws clutch at the clerestory attempting egress;
their compound eyes roll blind at the apse.
Another take: pan zoom lower the boom and
now empty sprockets whine in filmless cameras.
Sirens blare for saran gas.
The expectantly reverent lay wreaths at manhole covers
vermillion paper buddy poppies grow from ventilations
below the klieg-lit buttresses, another shadow trembles past
where the sensually charismatic scourge bright scallops from
one another's' backs.

Distance and time
rut and riot
twitching bellies, pelvi humping-upwards receive the smoke
peritonea rearing-up receive the holy service
at once trap doors open and windows shut
the nude are trucked tattooed conveyed incinerated
all the bodies kept in parenthesis until the moment of denial.

Distance and time
with no one rising from a grave, no one searching for a grail
this is no apocalypse
no evil over which to triumph
when days are numbered,
and, as I've warned you, numbers are coming up.

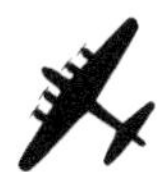

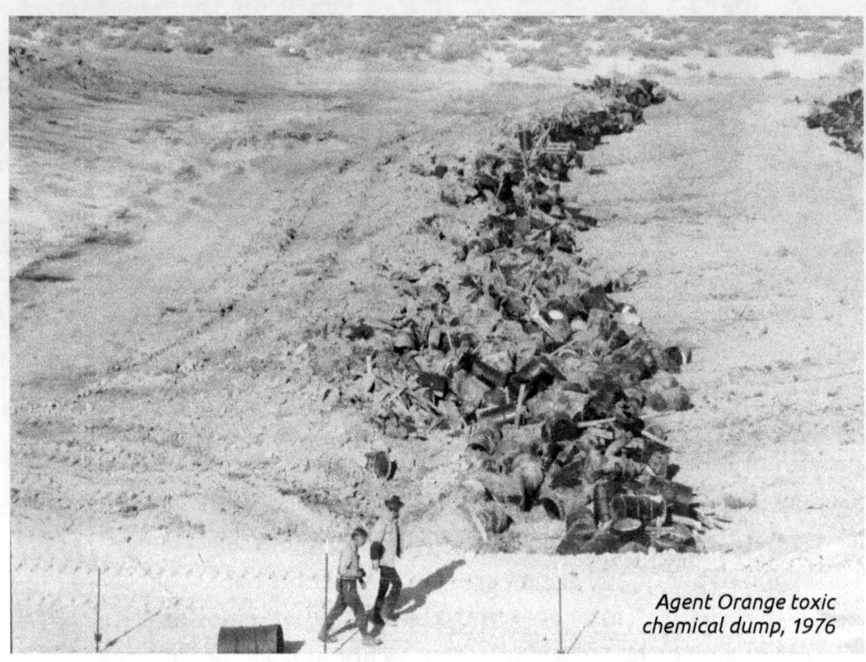

Agent Orange toxic chemical dump, 1976

With that certain uncertain feeling of nausea
this is a tale of the killing ground, the most noxious
creosol and deteriorated barrels, at dead noon as
frightening as the very still calendar hanging in front
of me as whole flocks of wounded white birds fall
into this bloodied sunset.

Along the smoldering seafront, dolorous eyes kept from sight
by the blue corpses of their fluttering eyelids
with loads of withered skins, crewless trains throbbing
in darkened depots with their incessant shunting
in breathtaking ink.
And then the moon was a perforated ulcer with that
insanely bright smile showing through as the most hideous visage

lying in wait for us, and dying to
wait on us is this three headed dog of
total darkness.

Don't tell me you have nothing to do!
Truth is feeble only in cities' cathedrals where
the business man screams for his highly paid assassin;
the politician pours acid down the throat of his new lover;
the virgin lies under the all black dream of searching roots
the soldier masturbates as though cleaning his rifle.

Don't tell me it's cold!
Let the sun pierce your body with
yellow arrows.
Let lichen grow under the frost.
Let lichens expand their crimson.
Careful! Let the rearrangement of rocks become humus,
and forest be here when the prairie falcon come back
to find her white streaked ledge when the lake becomes
spring and blooms pea green with algae.

Don't ask me for the time; time is all around, it's even underground.
Soft seepage staring with cold eyes.
The sun burns your heart.
The moon settles alongside
your great longing,
waiting for us to become human.

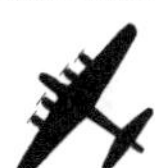

Beneath the rift, adrift within night's dark perceptions,
I glimpse the pariah's white teeth; irises in undulation,
the yellow eyes are a turning owl's face and seated at the
brooding tree is a hermit tending his sleeping flowers;
noting our presence, this huddled figure in near darkness, in the shift,
the light, the night, the black sand sifts into contemplation
shaped the way a furtive shadow motions.

The truth is somewhere, out there unknown.
Light was chirping in summer's valley,
but its the dull thudding in winter we remember,
the dreaming bodies thrown end-long upon the snow,
chewing their own tongues, coughing up their lungs,
this sputum and cacophony of machine guns;
in later days in the future-scape, a bellowing horizon raining pyroclasts,
the black ejaculate stiffens, becoming rack and ruin with cuprous odor,
its violet glass the color of manganese,
color of a quaking world with igniting trees
and man and woman on their knees endure yet another active inunda-
tion—
vast bowels vent molten bolae, holes recanalize in sudden gas
and heavy fall, the soft ovoids cover the smoldering boles
of a mythical forest.

And we remain; we regain;
deep, deep in spasmic water,
in red fringed acid, we are reborn,
from between the rugal folds.

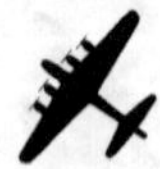

From somewhere
plays the descant commentary of wild geese
which became obsessional and minimalistic
and somewhat too long
with the upper voice.
The conductor, now maddened, throttles our century
with the music of the heavy machine guns,
picotage and mitrailleuse.
And here is our wealth,
the barrels in clusters
each with bright and bold Spitzer paints,
cairn coherent in link belts folded into
coffin boxes with handles for easy portage.

Given the surplus
you may have one of your own to own
but take care where you stand
these are jagged thigh bones
that pave the ground.

Time is rife, commiserative and ripe
but the vibrant voices have joined with
unusual tremolo and geese's eyes, pizzicato,
are small but very critical
when our bones emerge like locust searching,
they may in passing devour all
in the much-needed finale
as the score demands.

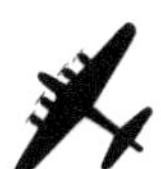

Complaint is the strong voice
of even the smallest bird
at this most ruined landscape.
Nowhere is a prize for uncommon courtesy
a common currency, where sorrow
with uncountable arms
and lashing clouds and the most creative deity
dance on the child of ignorance.

I too could become one with the sea,
one of the missing.
I am afraid of falling or falling asleep.
But today I saw one
thousand tundra swans
going north,
and they saw me, those wondrous ones
in search of a god.
I would like to go with them.

Nothing but time endures for eternity
the playing card torn in half,
yours and mine.
This is the room we played in for all its worth.
We sought and took and then we left.
A cracked plate under the geranium.
We left the joker in laughter, face down,

But the other half will play out,
tomorrow,
at the end of time, yours and mine
parce que
les jeux sont faits.

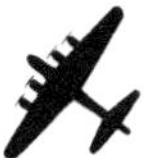

But the planet stays its course,
ozone or no. The restless striving
between birth and death, spasm and collapse,
with not a yard to plant a foot,
not a square to call one's own.

The paid liar is the rank halitosis
of the new world order.
The whoring of industry
is a new breed of cat, fat or otherwise.
Man, the sex-crazed mammal,
Kneels, bows, falls prostrate,
to that god everyone knows and blows.

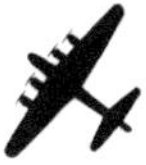

Danse Macabre

"Per me si va tra la perduta gente."
religion and drugs religion and drugs.
Everyone is whore and everyone is monger.
"Wouldn't you linger a bit longer—have the waiter pour another cup?"
Our lady of Pleasure arrives and takes the seat across,
sliced fruit are smiling lips; the face with no other features
face erased in makeup.
"Didn't you hear? We hear trained shrieking
through the flower papered walls
and the singing obscene, the danse macabre.

Everyone with lesions hungers for cures and salvation
but all specifics were disallowed by specific regulations
hearts are allowed, however
offered to the sun after the Aztec manner,
micro-liths—the micro-surgeons become the
official practitioners at Final Rites
knowing where the money is and glad to be of use.

At the last dinner
stubborn masks cover deceitful faces
harlequins and totem clowns compete under deceiving eaves
and the chimneys are falling down to fading streets.
That one dressed as a stag hurries away in his final day
his last sniggering, his last dance in cave light.

This city floats up against its own dark reflection
with its miasmas wailing, rising
becoming acrid clouds floating away
beyond the walls and
asylum doors, the groping crowds,
the voices stilled
the chemicals killed.
One more day, dead birds rain down.
The unloved peregrine in its deadly stoop
falls from grace
in this final day of Moloch.

At the beginning of our tenure
in surrealist coliseum sumptuously padded
with the shaved hair of millions
on a wooden erection built from a manger
trained dogs queue to fornicate the bound virgin.
At orgasm each falls frothing in rabid spasm
the virgin impassive on her knees
the conception immaculate as conceived.
We who are about to die hail thee, Caesar.
In nomini patris et filius et spiritus,
we sanctify your name.

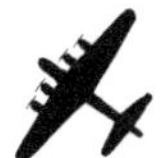

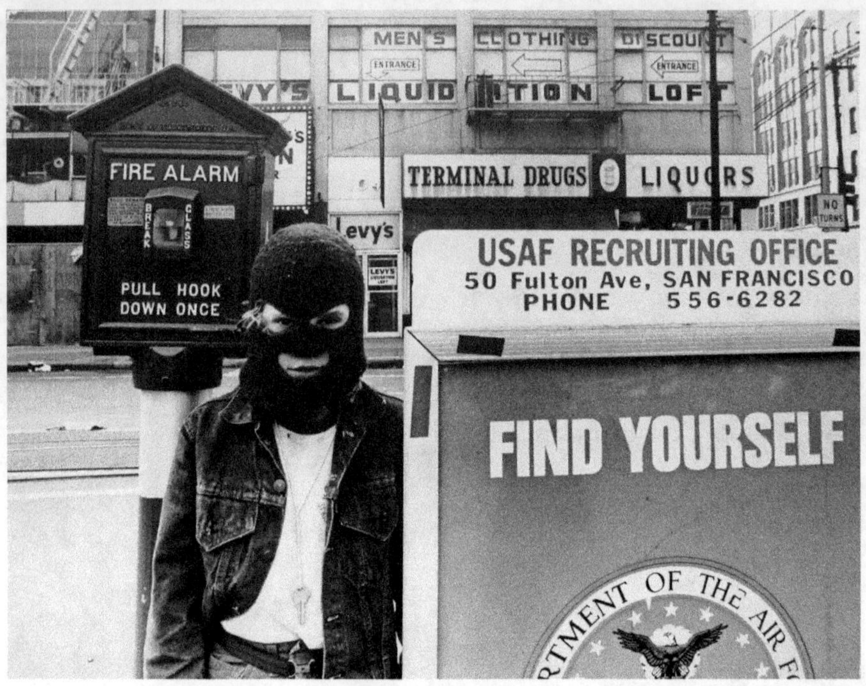

Don't you get it? There's nothing to get when there is nothing!
Then to disappear into terminal darkness where all time is mute.
God is man, man is God.
Bright light or the twilight that reveals bared teeth.
Must I chase one or the other, or must I die like an angry badger
praying for a future that is futureless
passing faces that are featureless
as the sky dumps its load of gravid rain.

The ultimate vulture,
the noxious answer,
the weight of what fails.
Did you really want to die with every sunset?
Did you know that every dawn looks like a sunset?
Such greedy wishes throwing coins into the fountain of blood
in a famished land where prey has vanished.

All these stones I have worn down to bring them up anew
from under that slow, slow glacier that seems to be my only voice.
The wind's jaggedness about these entrails and upthrusts,
the wind, as old as an entr'act,
calms the corridor's door.
Not flood, not even blood can shake the blood thirst.
Now the steady state has found a new voice
and with it an old word: Folly!

Hands cupped upon the eyes to see no evil,
Hands open, the mask opens and the eyes within see no evil,
The mask closes to see no evil.

In the end the sea has washed up
here on this revelatory beach,
as its own victim.
Please don't ask me how we should live
ask how we have.

Again last night I plundered my own works
and found something nearly understandable
lately chiseled into pink porphyry.
How pretty, but how ominous the rumbling.
The anxiety of this new generation that struggles
through grey schists,
hot rugia, yearning to be born upward
onto the dying planet.
Could one expect them to eschew
the usual nonsense
about an immortal soul?

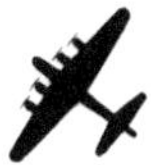

Doubtful is man's role in the universe
doubtless nothing beyond his self-aggrandizement.
If his sun winked out tomorrow,
nothing in the cosmos would look for it.
No one would listen for all that noise he made
pulverizing a small planet.

Hollow eyed, we cannot describe
the Mafia in congress with the Senate,
Tellurians praying on their knees.
In the upper world Congress is congressing
with the rank organs of the underworld.
Cernunnos rages, stamps his cloven feet
and semen puddles dry on the Senate seat.
Adam's nervous apple can barely speak.

In the rightful upper world
hellbuster is crackerbuster
and no one the wiser.
Alumni on their praying knees
Sex for hire, sire.
Are lovers offended by one another's odors,
hell-bent orders, and essential scent?
With withered blackened feet,
harlequin death in white face
dances in our septic gardens.
Cyclic tides range beyond the phrase;
words rush as waves, collide against
the periods and periodic shores.

During these years of mindlessness
and ever more willful—starvation, hunger,
I am even stronger.
Victim of the age this is my life.
Beyond the red light
a puffed up cloud born behind
the traffic light, now green
and time to go, time to go.

Save yourself, but I sense hell here.
I renounce all.
I start again.
This escape is my rebirth,
and you are reborn with me.
The clouds and prairie falcons shelter us;
blue heaven is our renaissance.

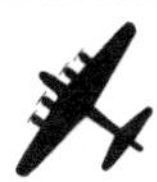

For the first time we are buying time
as ozone yawns in azure erasure
in flawed silence a sonic boom makes scree slide,
screech owl hide, wild dogs howl.
As hopeless afterward the desert finch reechoes
its glittering tropes from canyon walls,
but now as I listen to the wind cry out,
and put my ear to the ground,
it sounds more and more like profanity.

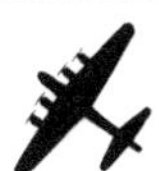

Guessing that acts are acts of consequence
or consequence depends on act
or consequence descends from act,
all grumble off together
belligerently to their fecal wallow,
snooze the grand excretal dream
the cloacal chorus grunting
"Our product is progress."
And puffing from rotundas gelatinous lips form words
as audible edibles sounding reasonable squealing, "Although ruin
ruins all, this is necessary to the common weal and the national
security and ummmm...the well being of all..."

Ravens though ravenous cry the truth in single syllables.

Do you remember?
In the beginning was the Word and the Word was with God.
Thot the ibis headed Word of Isis
and Word is God: the Word conceived in semen
born in blood.
"I am He who fathers sending seed," He said.
"This universe the womb is where I plant seeds
of all life," He said.
The sperm cells one woman can hold are so many
enough to populate the galaxy even though sparsely, I said.

Yes, the Word women powered
the Word spoken with the tongue thirst thickened
liquid loosens.
The tongue lets fall the Word from lips grown thin
in anger, looser, lush in love,
lets fall the Word that quavers before the galaxy
our destiny: the whispered Word fluent on tongues
effluent in currents among obstinate stones
the hard daily facts
moved, rolled and worn smooth in the torrent
gentled southward in a living stream.

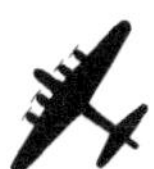

Lawns, trees and the forty eight bell carillon carried on the bay breeze,
Are crowded out by iniquitous asphalt and the nation's chlorination,
    benzene and phenol.
None know as much as should be known in the last encounter,
in the last calendar year, with disrupting eruptions and weapons in of-
    fensive mode.
I watch the mountains tumidity and monitor the backs of my hands yel-
    lowing tendons;
Skin becomes transparent as I become invisible.

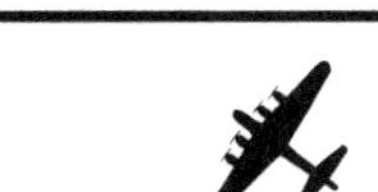

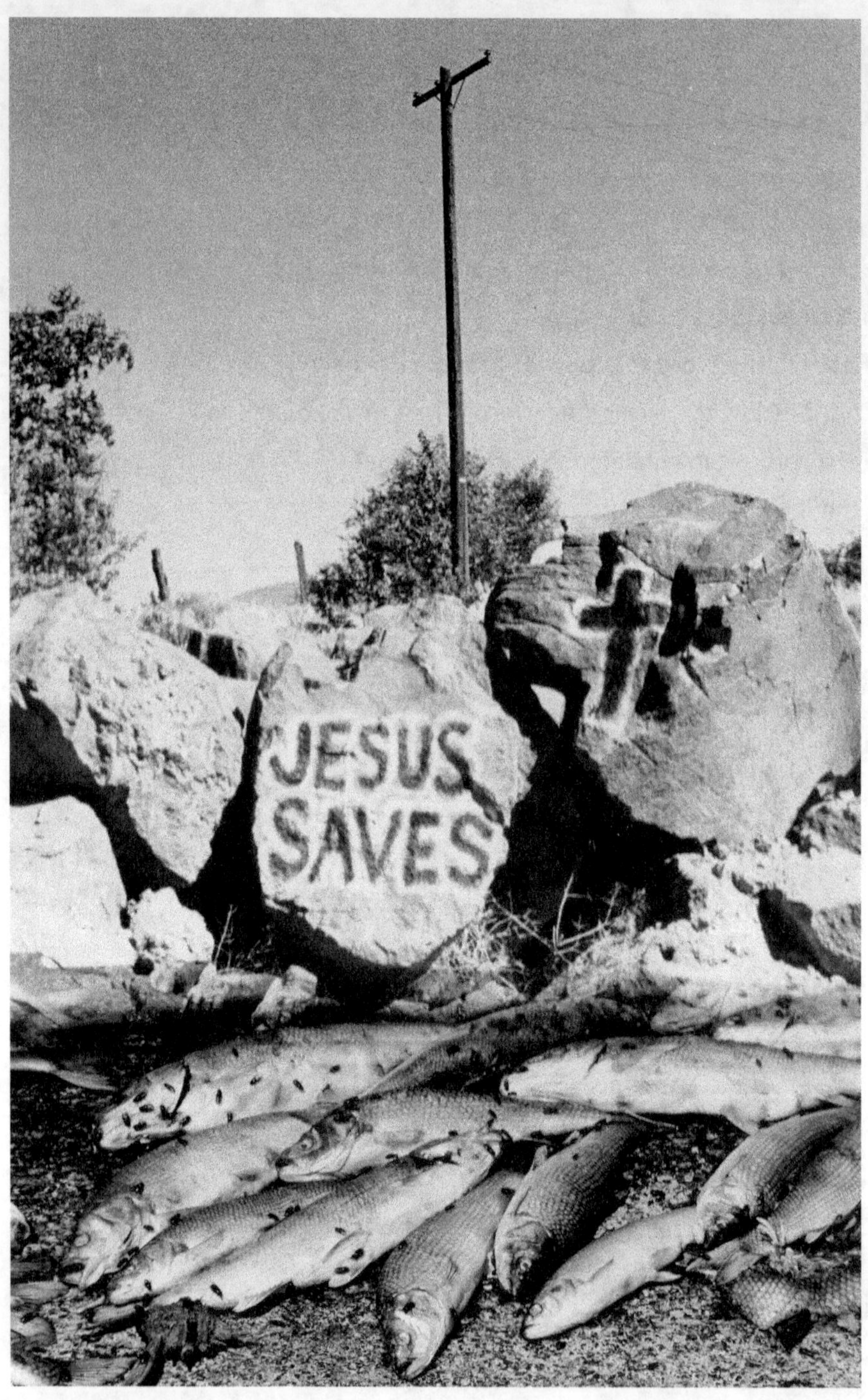
JESUS
SAVES

His final inscription chiseled in the bunker wall—
This was civilization, for all that it was worth—

Beauty in birth, beauty in death—
never were the sunsets redder.
When the last of the magi
raves his simple-minded gospels
to the complacent hills
with his sputtering spray can,
paints the word on the holy stone
in plain sight of the riant rim rocks—
Jesus Saves.

When the last servant of the people explains
to the relentless lens of abandoned television:
there is no imminent danger,
then will deities of man and men
be banished to another world, to this desert,
to their last rewards, their just desserts.

Here I shall wait, tending the stone,
beauty washed in the same blood.
Late saints and scholars
forget themselves
and masturbate on the public steps,
cry for lost hills where they
used to fall in deep grass
divining stars all night.

...cont.

...cont from pg 171

Hills are gone to condominiums
and hard macadam streets,
their junipers dressed and cowed
balled and prostrate.
Hucksters and shills, finding few buyers,
hawk wares which only lunatics could dream up.

Who would imagine
that our restlessness could atomize our bones
and unseat our world from orbit?

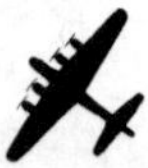

Listen to me as I sleep
hunched at the outermost shoals
of the dreamer's dream.
Mine, a famine of mind, given the times.
My work seems to be to pollute the immaculate.
Mine is an arduous gnawing,
this greater rumbling in argument
from under the ocean—long cracks aflame.
On the ocean bed
new lava pushes up its black pillows.

At the edge, I was sent to find what the wind did.
Blindfolded to learn the rifle,
so many of my friends out of fear and fatigue

have made their peace in body bags.
In the dust, the odor of blood,
and the sign of murder over the ocher
with little left of rut and love.
Here the dead dream of nothing more than
their postures in the aggregate.

The sign is grey ash strewn all the way
to Norway and beyond to redder sunsets, sunrises.
This raw wind as rough as the escarpment
was a spell which came upon me unaware,
an instinct with the taste of lizards and lichens.
This wind which brings to the overcast
three deep troughs of condemnation.
This wind over each man's world as tangible as mine,
this wind from across a wild-scape of understanding,
set with boulders, larger and older,
standing as elders under the same spell,
piled in a cumulus sky.

The autumn cloud's clean skein
catches the swallows violet passage,
a nostalgia which stirs the asters,
stallions in the wide pasture,
their shadows like lions stalk the nervous foothills.

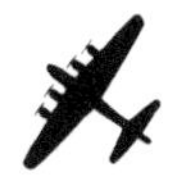

All the trees of mystery have been felled
and in startled silence one more bird flies away to nowhere.
Is that yet another chainsaw ripping the air?
Bare-legged circus girls, frozen smiles, a salesman hero harangue
defends his lectern and pompoms dance the sawdust;
it was he who long before warned me
not to criticize the Vietnam war.
In tedium a chain and wrecking ball
yet I'm trying to recall something
I said to that child who found the fallen
hummingbird's nest, the precious egg still in it
Where did she get it, where did she go?
I've looked everywhere in my mind;
it was the last chance and at the time I didn't know.

Birds— we watched the last flight, the blighted wings
over oblivion and at the obstinate mountain,
the coyote laughed derisively and once and for all
turned his face away.
Is a scarred mountain cenotaph enough?

Water gives up its fish, the dead stare,
bring maggots forth, in a multitude.
Wan creatures from the unrisen moon watch from the bars.
complain in gibberish diseases
in this city of no name.

Belly to back with thirsty whores,
we have all drunk long from the outfall and polluted shore
at the river of no name.
And the river yields up its blind: eyeless humans,
the kind fish have cleaned; all the soft inflations
held in by black wet suits (in negative buoyancy)—
killed our leaders, leftist bleeders, left us faceless,
to kneel in a drowned study, drifting down toward the mud
all testify in the name of the Lord.

Subpoenaed to testify, this one was shot nine times
in the mouth, a bleeding afterword, if not the last word,
finishes up the last words.
One was a fetus in a barrel before testimony,
and all the rest
rest in concrete with their
arms outstretched in wordless welcome.

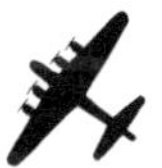

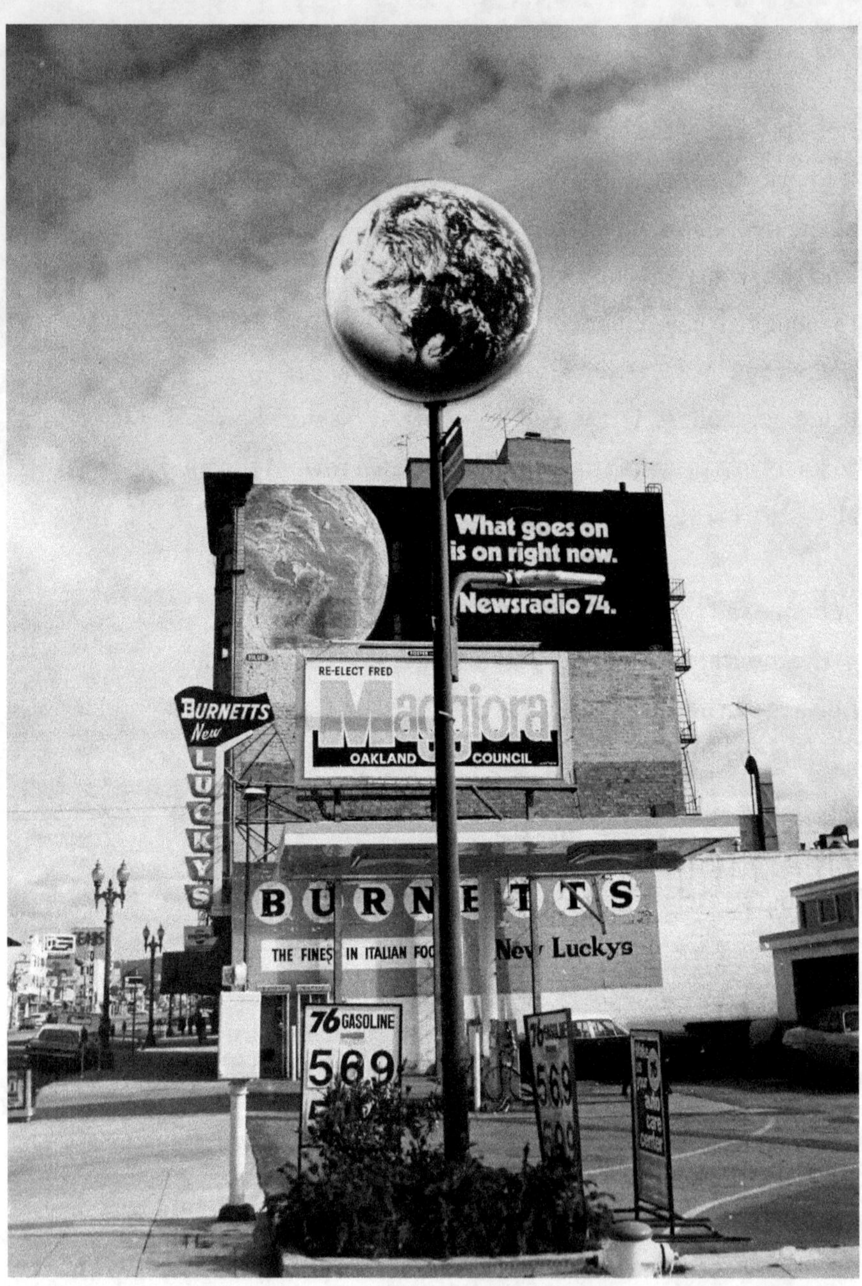
What goes on
is on right now.
Newsradio 74.
RE-ELECT FRED
Maggiora
OAKLAND
COUNCIL
BURNETTS
New
LUCKYS
BURNETTS
THE FINEST IN ITALIAN FOOD
New Luckys
76 GASOLINE
569

If it's all ongoing, please tell me what's going on!
Is the only thing left further deception and laughter
            like shattered glass?
Night slides between us and the false fronts.
Tomorrow's filled with nails which never were meant to hold.
What could you do if your world is as shallow as
Nietzche's was deep?

Stars poured through the window panes and filled his
room with an astonishing singularity.
Lost in indelible azure
in a dream it was promised that he
would meet Aletheia or was it Menippus but somehow
he knew he never could find either
along the white litora
where he knew scattered bones lay.
He would hold onto what was left but
his hands had already lost their grip
and his knees called out for support.
He had spent his years looking for the arcane
but never could get started because it was a secret.
Odd brown clouds suddenly formed like scabs
but there was a black void as absolute as zero.
Language finally failed him when he needed it most.

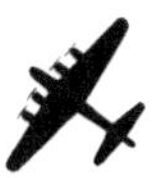

In a copper vessel, the discovery of the invisible
given the corrupt social order, the irrational is attractive.
Meanwhile, the earth casts up the sun as we search for our place
in forgotten books, disquieting looks.
To rush forth in anger to wrest from dangerous holes our
struggling hopes
far more than ever we hoped for
then in a body we burst from the doors and smote the grass
for reason of its insistence
and our insecure stance.

I suggested the use of cadavers as models for icons or statues
of famous generals
for only the dead know the vulture's gentleness.
When all had finished speaking, I stood to listen
to our squandered prayers.
One at a time we stopped to lift the omentum to gaze upon
the omen—god's writhing frown.
Intractable, man has journeyed from knowledge to
ignorance because he ignores the knowledge.
I have drawn the umbilical as a spiral of birth and rebirth
under the sun's forgetful gaze,
and lest we forget,
I nail out to dry,
god's fresh flensed hide.

We pay out the line as in a labyrinth,
to pray at the dry outfalls
and culverts for increase.
All feet are punctured on the nails in the continuing ruins.

Blood robs me of my love, love robs me of my blood.
We are hunter folk in reconnaissance at the abyss.
Campfires of a strange tribe that range the stars
in a shower of bolides,
we found the cosmos, the indelible violet flower, edible.

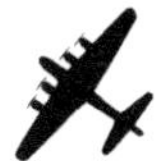

In the interlude between the wars
no new hope has emerged in the disquietude,
only raving and feverish nationalism.
Someone plays a dolorous violin; someone raids
the pay phone for lost words;
as the train throbs on the trestle, Valerie
becomes a butterfly.
Our new leader having such great desire,
but so little ability waits in the lobby;
attendant munitions wait in the bunkers.

Evening becomes a splendid sky shot through with meteors.
The changeless beauty is always changing.
I think of black fly hordes at rest in the night trees
dreaming of white maggots.
Here the fir is mute, the forest voiceless.
The crouching stones, the ageless is aging.
Man fights fate, fate fights man
As the wave shouts with the voice of man
the surf seethes with its drowning man.

Cri de falaise bafoue, au bas du soir
sous les cimes des houles, le lourd
mouette vire au blanche ver ses rives
vertes du naufrages.
Le bruit, la surdité, l'absurdité dans
l'abime de nos vies.

I stop here to wonder about the sagging cloud
its towering darkness, its grey weight
the street which used to be under it
and all the houses gone.

Unseen horses approach galloping but there is no bridge,
then on the black ridge where wild mahogany used to grow
lights begin: the new part of the sprawling town,
the new buildings already falling down.
And on the siding the train couples suddenly,
suddenly humps; a horse thumps.

I am told by the bell, hell is the place of perpetual
motion, constant clamor.
I am told by the bell from the Christian tower
we are not welcome here;
the birds tell me as the ruins grow.
The bell.

We must be smarter than dogs for our knowledge explains death,
death as the three headed dog awaits beyond our knowledge.
Something waits in the wreckage and we have lost something
beyond knowledge.
The bell tolling tells.
In the surf the voices swell.

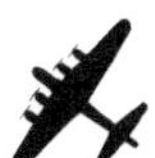

Inundated day
hemmed in by sheer cliffs of hatred,
cities of torment, washed marble vanity,
and concrete sand—their ongoing deceits.
Who in this hell were they, they who pulverized
the sacred shape, who exterminated love,
their origins, forests, and mutilated waters?

They who reside in their dangerous metals
toying with the stars trying the patience of
the most stoic stones?
The heart cries for those who try to sleep
in sinking dreams
annihilated stroke by stroke
by their useless works
and exaggerated colors.

What fires?
Was the adversary the institution?
But with each cessation of conflict
the sensation of a farscape strewn with wasted hours
and that growing from the wreckage was always the new age
replete with all the perceptual imperfections
complete with patient flowers
with their secrets of life locked in dungeons.

I imagine morning might become a hysterical radio
its emergency broadcast squalor
or the warning tones
of more shrieking dolphins.

The blameless spider in the basement window tending
shattered cobwebs
and more shock waves for the tender lovers.
Aftershocks tinder cities at ignition
and all small clouds with silver linings
will squirm and vanish to reappear again overhead
and everywhere over the very still earth and
not one bird will call again to the century.

I am marching uphill with the firs.
They know me well and
I touch them in recognition.
A forest.
Its just a matter of time.
This place will be made a desert
and no gods we dangle from wires
will be brought forth from the wings
to save the day from our heinous nightmares.

Of course I'm digressing with
that cloud, this thick smoke of ten thousand years
appearing, disappearing
in due course.
Oh, the sin list is endless and stretched about
the scandalous world many times.
Riotous winds, blushing clouds over riant rimrocks.

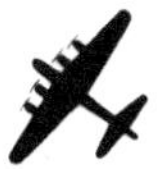

Is she here?
Why is she here?
Is it she who speaks
or is it someone or no one?
You are speaking with my own broken words—
words that lie bleeding on the ground
and struggle to get up.
Know that all the tools I've gathered about my life
are damaged, and these eyes with which I watch you have
become pale holes which are fading into nothing.
Tell me why. Hurry, before I disappear.
She is moving. She's speaking.
Can you see the soldiers imitating
their own exhausted shadows?
Are you really here? Do you care?
Have you been here before?
No, you've never been here: to walk with me
through white ashes made of nothing more than noise.

I do care. I do care. Incline your ear and listen
from the far corners: emotion with strident voice
commotion with bloodied face and the death squad comes forth
to prey once more upon its own.
Little more than smoke protects their nakedness,
so habituated to life, the dying make very bad deals
with their obsessions, confessions, adhesions.
Look what the dead have done.

I can ask you what you've done for the dead and done for:
I've done nothing; nothing waits beyond the angled black
and beyond the billows.
Street signs are the crucifixes.
An ancient people from a once impacted city flee
through tombal streets, inclining smoke, guttering fires,
piled tires, the barricade.

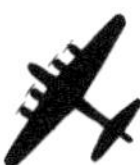

Nothing left behind, nothing saved.
Nothing I own, I renounce all;
I start again, here, far in this solitude,
wasteland without life save our own.
And you with me, without country
or race, joined by plight and mystery.
Desert falcons cover us!
Shelter us! We are both elect and the prey.
Such foreboding and hope in barren dust.
Rebirth is renaissance!!
Mother, we are of your water.
The Sun, our father. We are created from your flesh
and your own shriveling heat.

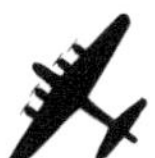

Persecuted by my dreams and tissues of the awful,
throttled by my own words...
far fangs and scarlet clouds racked
against awesome dentition,
bed of hunger, tooth of doubt: weather chews
new shape at the distant edge about the nights
first showing in the tattered sky bleeding.
I flush at what I see; I pale with what I feel.
I have signed my name in the crust, thus endorsing
the work, making the whole goddamned barren land,
my found object.
But stay;
Witness!
I am doing something!
Something!

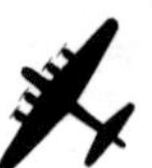

Like ashes that lie in abandoned piles
I smolder at night 'til dawn,
hoping to be revived.

Someone comes in asking questions
describing morning as storm,
fright appears as a long grey
cloud that never ends,

small quick shadows that cross the hills,
like contour lines, all head in
the same direction.
A bluff shrouded in black
which is unseen until it's too late,
and it's always too late.

I've been speaking on the subject of injustice.
One could listen through the paucity
in my chest—
I am slurred,
hard to understand,
but always right and the
Christ mongers know it.
The insane lie,
the insanity that protects the lie.

Because shadows are fast and westering
and I am a shadow
of my former self,
I cry out like an ancient homunculus
carrying its blackened wings.

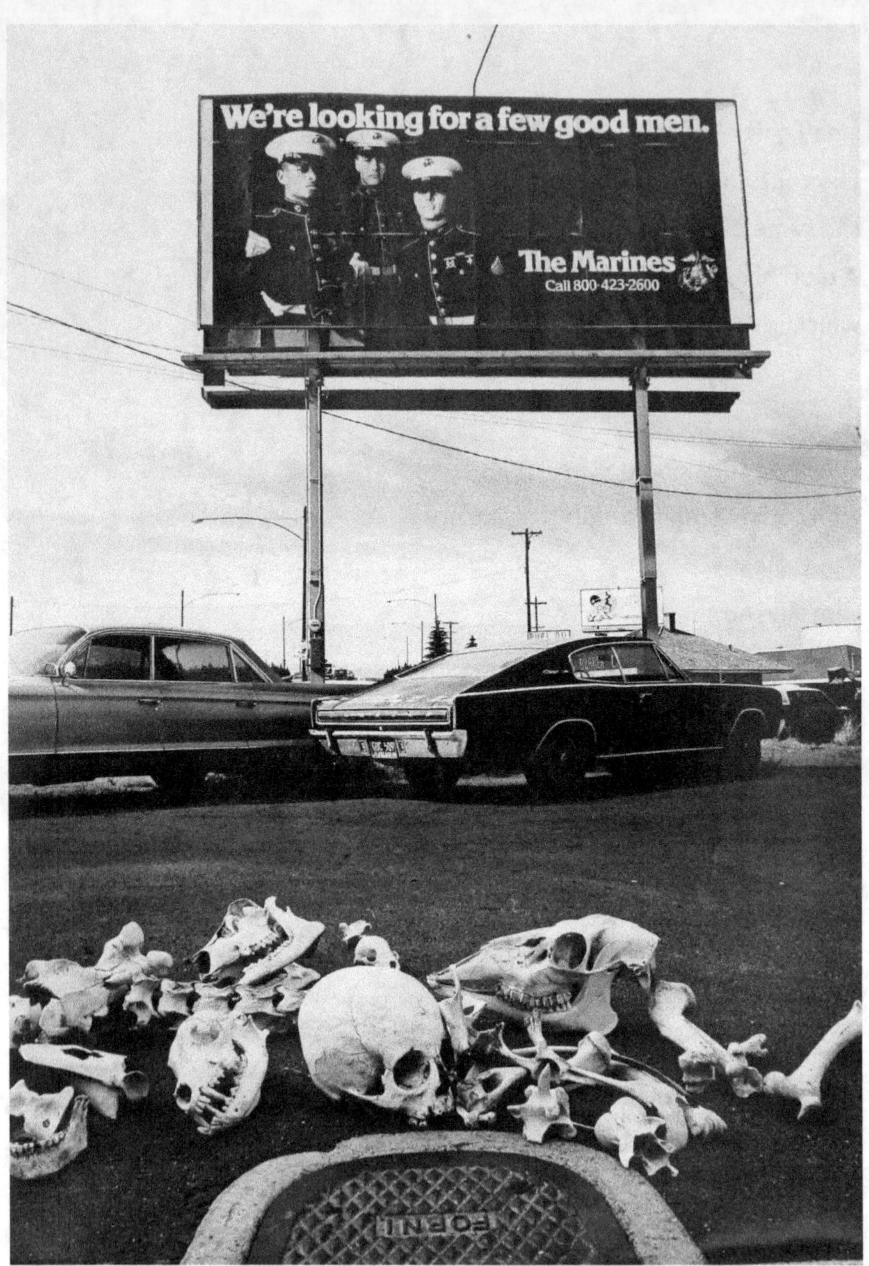
We're looking for a few good men.
The Marines
Call 800-423-2600

They're still looking for a few good men.
They had their eye on me a time past
when I was good man young and dumb
right for salvation training to whistles
and bells with soft and loudspeakers.
What's all that milling around in there?
We're counting heads and kicking ass.

They stuffed my body stranger than powder
into a canon breach and with lanyard yank,
the striker fell, the primer burst
but ignition failed nothing happened.
My fodder body wouldn't burn
the bones too brittle too little,
the skin too filled with arid moon.

Not such a good man after all, someone said.
Oh, I was extracted, not dead, brushed off
and reclassified, in red on the forehead
of my shameless face a cryptic, a military glyph,
meaning: "Non combustible."
Range, trajectory and breach pressure
"Not Applicable" was written somewhere in a file.

Jesus loves you.

Just a flash in the panchromatic
A click, a puff, a failure under the sun:
milling again and twitchy glances.

...cont.

...cont from pg 189

Willingly, dressed and covered
in splendid epiphany the next in line
was loaded locked in a caught breath
the striker fell straight through
his paper soul leaving a rectangular hole the shape
of his grave recorded by I B M as a card punched
a tiny coffin fell through.

Jesus loves you.

The furrow dug black and long
as the barrel ran back upon its grease and spring.
At the muzzle quick flower gray, orange and black
or the red, white and blue with joy
beyond decibel measurement
that jumped the nuts, stunned the lungs
brought snot to the nose, tears to the eyes
tore an acrid hole through heaven and a cloud
with puffing, billowing pride
stamped on the forehead
for the unknown God and the decayed country.

Sweet Jesus did you know if you stand
behind the breach as I did
to sight along the barrel
when the shot fired as I saw it
the body may be seen as I've seen it:

at that very instant when all men
become the same color
burned black, fast flying?
The dull report answers
back from eternity:

Jesus SAVES.

The search goes on for a few good men.
A few is all that it takes
for instant apotheosis,
the military recipe for immortality.

I'm watching those who watch me now
and know I've missed my loading
calling for a few good men for
selected sacrifice
like the selected ones posing in the
poster digging traffic slipping by
on slick hype and Arabian grease.

I'm thinking of spring:
of day lilies orange and black;
the quiet blooms that open slowly
and last and last, if only for a day.

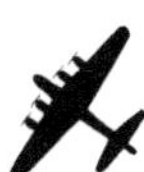

Fetal figs twist on their dry twigs,
wither as they cry.
Depravity. This century winds down,
rolls to its end, a century of prating
strutting troops and liars, the prisoners,
the inexplicably sinister evil elite.

Monstrous flowers and unbidden waters,
then pellucid, now heuristic but a serious
threat—peloria at the mowing—our esoteric
brothers in their corridors of power ignore
the past, refuse the future.

Note the drama: the beauty, Hebe, comes bearing
her cup...
Hecatomb at the insistent diorama:
with blunted brushes hell kites paint the large scale
slaughter and we are waiting in trauma,
in vain, trembling in humility.
Isn't it wonderful how meek the diabolical
when standing on their knees; these starveling
olive trees scatter their useful leaves in despair.

Can I stave off the ennui and that spermaceti
in its awesome rankness that washes against my indolence?
I languish cancerous, dressed to the hilt
prating much about spent shadows.
And, I worry about this shoreline trace this all but vanished
high water mark of three thousand years.
Oh, what of our shores?

My appetencies are quickening at the Satyr play.
Your lovers crowd me in our bed expanding their
eager appetites and there is no room left to keep
the death watch.

Gentle Hertha unrolls her deer skin, spreads
out her herthe at the hearth.
as we watch
vulture death keep its ultimate rendezvous with
the entire race, falling in fell swoop.

What! Are you, too, in search of clavicles and
these small stones of great meaning?
We have waited a long time for this day and
this is the day. Stroll once around this shore,
mirrored in the lake, we are seen as we are;
sit at this rock, and vultures take us for what
we are; but, we shall endure
until keeping our heads up is too hard a task.

Yes, of course, I want to read it all in the final
reports, all about the concocted evil in tubes and retorts
—Pan, zoom, time lapse... Report!

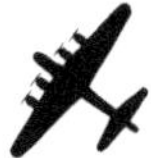

Not even wild camels could tolerate
the gaze of pitiless stars for long, desert so devoid,
this deserted earth as we know it,
this void so much like galactic sand.
Not that land, part of unremembered eternity
peopled by dreams
but this one patrolled by armies as if blood were infinite.

Tell me if you've learned these strategies of sand
the hopeless beauty of ceaseless, restless sastrugi.
Tell me so that we both might understand it.
Give me the meaning of those lips in eternal motion.
What is said on those cosmic mouths that sound like voices
au secour with the lifelines trailing from crewless ships?

Here the wind taunts with strange unbearable sounds
like love lines and violins if they could be
heard above the silence.
This is the candle burning and not for long.
These are the withered and castaway stumps
of the trees which shone where the sea
thrashes in its death throes
to cast up its bloated dead.

Sharp knives slice under soft throats
the weak candles in processional darkness.

Struggling to get up, we aren't quite
aware that our backs are broken.
Surrounded by death,
we never guessed what it meant.

Remembering my childhood is looking
through trellises beyond rose thorns
which prevented climbing
and preying mantises—give us this day—
which to this day wander
and posture in my thoughts.

Cohorts! Robots!
Cash in your scruples!
Make tender illegal!
Hatred in their eyes—
the game is catch a fool.

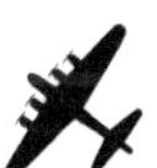

Of a sudden a blinding espalier, the black lapse,
then the roar upon the worried mountain's brow,
a forked sign raked across all crania,
the crabbed line wrinkled like an ancient face
in judgment, just distinguishable
in the alternate iridescence.

Because the orchard is again heavy with fruit,
as is its habit, the new race already bristles with metal
when drums sound in nothingness;
already legions are on the roads to nowhere
and one more chapter lies open in this great book of stone.

My thoughts along these lines
keep their vigil in the amethyst stria where I hold you
there at the purple edge under my strong hands
and the gifted sight of arctic falcons.
I shall force you to see it—your feet at the edge
of the sorrowful canyon, its hanging blue steel
on the slope of the crevasse,
with its sad melt water rushing upon all things human.

You would see it, and I have held you to my promise.
Again I am left at the turn in the street
where first I was called
by a tonsured crowd faceless,
necks in iron rings.

I am standing again in the wind,
which ends in the usual blind alley.

I have awakened in the orans posture
on the other side of the world,
within the water at its end
in a submerged city inhabited by the great shark
where a placid octopus shakes in the jaws
of the insatiable moray.

Here, I have found these dead lead soldiers
from that other generation,
but I find nothing of the fur seals on the ice pack
except their trustful brown eyes,
heedless of the approaching army,
swinging bloody clubs.

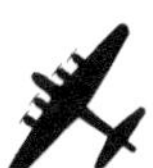

And settling into my old habit, I let my mind sink
into its own havoc, hag-driven, where pulse remains pounding.
And here we are at the last threshold,
perturbations, maledictions, derelictions in duty.

And the ridge where the cougar lies dangerously in the
sun, its rosettes hidden by adulthood, now doomed due to
its spots. A few bird calls, mocking
and in a time of mud, rain, and ash, if anyone be left
to remember, for what would we be remembered?

I was here in my youth dreaming with a drawn bow string
considering the seasons.
Now hell's drowned out every sound and floods the new age
with new breeds.

Yes, I think the sun has grown tired of us:
great spots and flares have newly formed; drought and
insanity sets in; we shall ring in the new age and then
extinguish in the last bright blink at the hottest peak
of fulguration.

The magenta rock rose full-blown, blows;
its petals ornament violet corpses,
blown by the most common
of houseflies.

Send the message; the alloy is nearly ready;
listen, lean closer; set it down page by page.
Problem without solution, we examine the cause
because wasn't it obvious we could have
obviated the cause?

The end, the action ends; bloodshed at the time of
word-shed, a time of last times and ponderous songs.
It is here we shall wait until the last scholar puts
down his final pages, executes his ultimate inscription.
I sit with the widow and her weeds and ashes,
I have conquered the ugly, subjugated
the beautiful. Joining the two, I abide in the middle in the
wash of words, watching the fire.

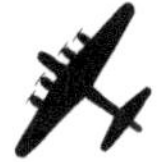

The sanctus bell rings a salutation to
latter day daguerreotypes.
What was it that betrayed us? The great floods
of the last century betrayed the vast silence—epochs of grass,
the songs of wandering poets maundering about
their dreams and their lost women,
their bones and moons.

I have said goodbye to the world before, yet I remain
to take charge of myself at last and now
it's welling up again, the green wave,
coming on strong with swans riding, kenning,
this song of Oregon sung to those
who know its dense mountain cover and cryptic geologies,
you who celebrate the world primordial, our origins
our grey stones, our wide margins.

As the ancients mourned in mutilation, cast out
their precious stores at the passing of their kindred
at the fresh graves, slaying every kine
anointing their horns, horns of the King, with crisma
slit throats of their beloved rams, crying Kristos eukeros.

In terror, listen to the world's utter stillness
as the mauve sky deepens.
The hours beat from the silent drum,
iron rust is reddening.
On severed tracks where trains wait on time.

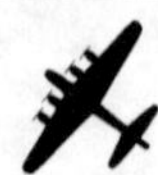

The sky is falling!
No, it is only evening falling,
as if the dawn gave up
each shadow's dreadful secret
or down each threatening passage
between sentinel rocks and quaking aspen
nothing might be saved from night
before the reds collapse
and the sky comes in upon itself
when wind gives over to velocity
and that will happen because I know
the weather's mind.
Tricky men
have tricked the earth
out of silence.
The sound of horrendous ending
and terrifying surrender
before another question could be asked.

Dedicated to Russian Lieutenant Colonel Stanislav Petrov (Sept. 26, 1983), who courageously chose not to provoke retaliation and destroy the world when atmospheric aberrations looked as if America had launched a pre-emptive strike against the Soviet Union.

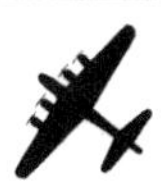

The Sin List

Something is missing; lost at the crossing,
limping with bleeding boots across infected earth
and a captain strangles Asia's daughter.
His smile betrays his hands to the astounded visitor.
Avenge his treachery!

Eat the flesh of sons served nicely at the banquet;
then toast the encroachment.
Eyes idle on the distant cliff, the cries agonized.
This is amphibole with jeweled inclusions of basalt columns—
amygdaloidal with agatized eyes,
squinting in the mass.

Our heroes are elsewhere,
somewhere in eternity, a dreary land missing its trees—
but again I stroll too far in a grimacing dream
missing its teeth.

Astounding vines choke mimosa,
and birds court with tails the shape of music.
And black earth cast up war's art,
yet flat enough between the craters to land a helicopter.

At the trail, alongside, we take up the sleep watch
with lions and gypsies, find hapless feathers,
the snares, their spans entwined, indifferent to species.

The sky with fast crowds gathering,
lightning with sound like the rumble of bowels,
a dull pain, a flaring obsidian with yellow sulfur,
a canyon loaded with profane commentary.
The scandal caused rocks to crack,
when truth revealed itself in the fractures.

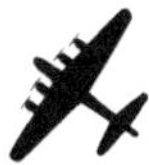

The distance lights the evening cliffs,
severe desert.
With tripod and camera
I have taken a position.
I have cocked the shutter;
I shoot and the gray sod
jumps with the detonation.
The projectile
rushes into the twilight sky
with the sound of trains passing
in a tunnel.

No blue flash of lens and Olympus,
no sparseness inflamed in a vast periphery.
Shock waves, the great hiatus,
as the awful cloud makes for a
nearby city to catch its distinguished
gentlemen after dinner,
gaping upward
at the extinguished colors.

Tomorrow I should work
with the ocean's most fecund green—
make it boil and steam,
as it did in the very beginning.

I photograph clouds and leaning trees
and factories with dripping snouts,
The shadows that loosen all shingles
and swallow entire crowds.

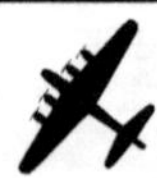

The river rolls where sink worn tires,
where floats factory effluvia
of the most dangerous kind,
and the bird at the bearded bank,
the most beautiful, showing only his
color from within the reeds.
Or was it the whisper from
the moon's faun-spotted face
in its worried lunation
over this dying rind,
an avocado wrinkled, drying out?

At dawn we keep vigil just within the door
with our women, with wan smiles
and with knowledge of their tumors.

And the conclusion rests on the premise
which itself depends on the conclusion
or, as we have seen,
the solution gives rise to another solution
which brings forth again the *a priori.*

The laws concern clean air, clean water,
but this poisoned river runs with blood
pumped from the gills of struggling fish.
The hardiest bass search the depletions and
the delicate trout settle with the patient mullet.
There, that flash in the lion's eyes is only hunger.
And just beyond those rushes are stags
with eyes softer than my mother's.

With our babies in billions we have prepared
very well our huge bed of slaughter.
A flayed victim splayed upon the stone,
a whole world watching and no one the wiser.

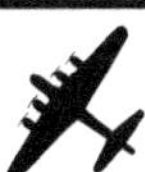

"Man is the measure of everything." -Pythagoras

So again you've caught me in this slate place
which reveals its secrets in the laminae
where tireless blue was compressed, no, composed
by uncountable ignitions in dense solitude.
Here metamorphic rock was composed
by ancient lives burnt out in round red marks
like myriad kisses.

How hours ache.
How many times has the moon
cast its hourglass on
this sleepless lake?

Love and terror:
These grebes that mate at midnight,
Whose voices move the roots of my hair.

Does anyone speak?
No! No one speaks.
No one.
Man speaks for no one;
no one has spoken for man.

Because this boon we thought was good
was evil,
evil became destruction.
The anguished light collapsed
just as language lapsed.

This is the lacuna of the future,
sign of non-existence.
Man is the measure of nothing;
nothing the measure for man.

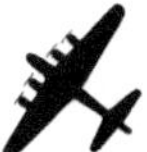

Tradition Dies Hard

With sour hearts and mourning words, tradition dies hard.
Campfires kill the sclera, tumors blinding,
tradition clings like practice.
Finding the most vulnerable parts, day fails.
Tarnished light and colors erase around us.
Eyes, moon-blind, renunciation and drone. Only the
most desperate secrets can surprise the not-yet dead.

Clouds deluge in collision following the smallest stream.
We find an ocean with continuing conclusions and
there we pray to the clouds.
We lament in the din of the rivers warblers.
Rains displace the last dejected shadow
and the faun-spotted hills lie in the softness all around us.

Very still without odor near pools of pollen
dragonflies light upon the tide ponds.
Tomorrow the world's great entrails will lie in the sun,
smoking at the decisive moment.

...cont.

...cont from pg 207

Something more has been counted,
something already in the docile umber.
Hours slip from the five-fingered grasp of man
putting history in exile beyond our memory in
our vigil at the abyss,
amid soft symbols and muted flutes.

With every hour more species vanish
and I notice this small thing that prods my brain.
The same note from my earliest days again sounds
from noontide shadows,
so small and deceptive among
the blue-cast patterns on the sand
in suspense.

All of what we were is gone and
this that we are is fleeting
at the speed of birds.
With this self-same argument
I think I might consult with augury.

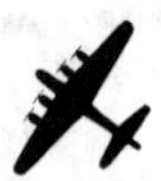

The west slides and the world slips
as relentless motion over the septic city
and the north star stares in fixity as the lessons
of the century drop from consciousness.

And it is we who are numerable positions on the curve
for this is the way knowledge is scattered
within the areas of great uncertainty.

We should take time out when the fix is in
because people are missing.
Bring to the fore when words have failed
the signal act of each other.
Each of them severally were entitled to receive
a future then perceived of time now seen to recede.

What river?
The river that knows our names,
the river that has always known our names
from loft to ditch It was a long way to Tipperary
but a short way to tyranny.
Bullets first perturbate, then freeze, then stop
hard within someone soft.

Heretofore, about which we've heard too little.
The vexed questions etched and echoing in abeyance,
intended to seek free exercise of speech.

And today I've found your eyes upturned in sand,
eyes ancient in antique polish
and I've fetched them, fisted, held close and expectant.
The ebb sockets filled with salt tears
in the flow all welling with millennial tears
beyond the sigh and swoon of galaxies.

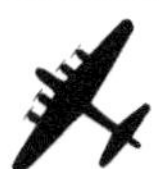

The stones in audience, birds in concert
with the awestruck sky—thus the mountains keep their
distance within the purple incantation spoken by me.

Nearly unnoticeable
another high altitude jet presses against the horizon.
Now the sound of constant droning
but I cannot guess from where it emanates.
I hear dirges edging forward
in the looming extinction.
From the ozone death whispers:
sharp harpoons fit for neither man nor beast
just like a whale, great with infant and dragging
harpoons, open wounds, tangled lines.
What contrails!

One part at a time: this time, the underside
with raised welts and the ragged part with white callosities
near the blind eye.

Fire and iron rather like orange colored candy
oozing, the sun melts upon the sutured horizon,
vanishes, risen in the future,
and the days pass to darkness
with sweeping nighthawks.

And nether man, banished to hard-featured country
ceaseless in dream, sleeps without knowledge:
the past has caught up.

As the surf devours the land
these wise-eyed gulls from everywhere see everything.
In the roiling amplifications at the eaten headland
combers in tiers gather to crash the troughs
to suck the hollows, a sound
which draws me near, nearer the fear.
Crabs in the frenzy hang on well enough

Nights filled with far cries
and words of the imperceptible
where darkness merges with first light
falls upon the surging wings of bright desire.
Aware that my body is the grave,
I call into question the necessity of building
another elaborate machine for god to ride in upon.

I have returned again to the steep path
and the crevices growing wider with winter
to these forbidden holes
the mud dauber fills with embalmed spiders.
Morning clouds drain eastward
as a slow leak,
their strictures sealing away the antlered sun.
Clouds drain eastward to that immense dimension
of men now mourning their last dementia.

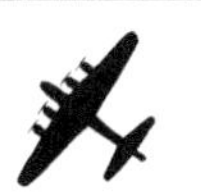

Things found out! Every stone has its secret.
Times I find myself in doubt,
but look, I'm coming down.
As I look down there from up here,
nothing is as it seems: principles and justice.
Night hawks jar the darkness, swooping,
and the ecstasy is intolerable.

During the lull—a nonce word for the occasion—
a rush toward the crush of bodies
to witness flames at the cease fire.
But, in the old days, (in *yeare iu*)
we were carried to death on our shields;
our bronze standards upright.
We left them on perfumed fields of crushed flowers,
or as castaways in iron chains
the ocean pulsing in their ears,
while we traveled half a lifetime
back to our thorn-tree forest
covered with trophies of the vanquished.

Nilotic melody at the longest river,
with nights heavy ebony, with noonless days.
In files across yellow sands,
we witnessed black beings stop to paint their melodic bodies
on the earth's abrupt abutment.

The ibis cries from the four directions and men answer.
birds answer with corrections,
and, at last, the melancholic mocking

by those who mimic birds.
Now be careful.

A long time—the agonized time,
the canonical hours in forbidden dreams,
I come across my libidinous women
spread-eagle across wild eyed horses,
refusing to speak, see, or hear
see nothing, hear nothing, say nothing.

And the sun fell a falling orange ball,
and burst into a thousand campfires on both shores.
Light in dreams of sleep, the off load falling on the weeping,
we change our mounts, proud necked, slavering at the bit exchange
another day wrinkles and collapses.
Sparsity, a spare sentence unknown and untranslatable.
Another world inhabited by calamity goes unnoticed
except for the women's great resentment.

Stalagmites, algae, magnificent cities,
full term metamorphosis,
as chrysalis of screw worms form and function.
There is no aftermath when it is simply over.
Existence has become exodus reaching up only to stoop so low.
Our words linger in the sacred yards,
bulls rumble in orchards afterwards.
We shall praise this place before we leave,
believe the holocaust has lost its cause.

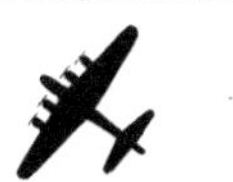

Trapped in a short life
I know I've lived a long time if dogs be there they bark.
The law has a bright face.
We polish our plates with ashes
smiling benignly here in eternity,
seven tapers of the menorah
symbolizing the last seven days.
Holy mother of god, pray for us sinners.
Hail, Mary full of grace.
Blessed is the fruit of thy womb.

Damnable contaminations, brightening conflagrations,
free of leprosy, clean or unclean as the case may be
always as the case may be with the blood at the four corners
the broken necks of hapless Semitic birds
covers the hiding intaglio, nexus plexus,
the awful ash at the well of wisdom.

Under these stars where the dead have left their flesh,
under those double moons of necrosis, this moth
covers us for a time, Cecropian eyes rising on its wings,
risen to the east across this night in which we lounge,
and for a time it might have appeared
that yet another lifetime would overtake us.

Getting off to such a dismal start brought us full circle.
And at the end of September that resembled summer,
we witnessed it written that something very interesting was seen:
although somewhat erased by nights with failed moons:
strange spots before our eyes
developed on the feverish ocean,

too soon after the waves without sound or motion,
stretched out soft grays to the dead.

See the earth as an oasis with the washed up dead at the shores,
the flock never returning to the hatchlings.
Few see the omen in that.
All colors in iridescence burn in the cloud of violet flies.
The tiniest motes sift in losing light, moonless night.
No sack as black, collapses.

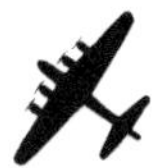

Oh, we were once aware of the slightest planetary perturbation.
Through civilizations oldest potsherds,
we shall amble heedless of dust,
without knowledge of memories,
back to our dark gardens,
gone to resurgent forests.
Language which once defended us, grumbling
in perverted dialect to the murdered species
could again comfort us.
We shall stumble out to the dangerous deserts
of experiment and sinister enterprise,
given over to the superstition and centipedes
only to find the pictographs fleeting shadows
scrawled across the inscribed stone,
initiatory symbols, birds and umbilicals,
the secrets set down by unknown tribes
in unremembered time of boon and favor
whispered of in faulty legend.
We shall ignore all meanings
and then deface our erasure.
We shall cull the fallen boulders for the true form of god
and proclaim once and for all, to improvident clouds:
all potholes his footprints.

The dawn, the dawn, await another dawn...

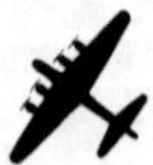

Aired in portly flatulence,
courtly flourish,
wild dogs rut our rabid trails. Backtracked without
advance, we glanced at heaven for a sign.
This shocking breeze is as fresh and surprising
as my first breath.

Now the last shrilling swine are led to common
slaughter, conveyed upside down by hooked hocks
to scalding water.
Attendants at the shoots—hard hats and hip boots:
everything is saved except the squeal.
Rank rivers are recanalized.
Hopeless in their iron collars,
the long files under fortified walls,
in an ever gaining line, a nation upon its feet
chained between the swinging catenaries
each at arm's length in an ever gaining column.
All ends in another emaciated day.
In the spider heat, the silk trees weep.

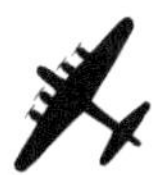

With surprise on our breaths, all reminded of apocalypse.
All eyes blinded, caught in the open, in the graphic-scape
engraved in the eye with double lightning flash
I dig into my quilt or into the erosion to repay the debt
through which all the centuries have eroded
to the edges of the most well-intentioned city, its glass
fronts, old golden mirrors in an evening dressed to kill.

This week it's time to prepare for our laughter.
The morality bungled. Compared to the scandal,
the vulture is beautiful.
So deep is the shame, stones of the Mayans lie face down
half covered by the jungle.

Thus is Aztec smoke. We were half awake when they
rushed down the slopes and were as quickly gone.
We were left to our puncture wounds no deeper than
frightened wombs, but enough.

But the law was with us and all the statues in
stone, those vast varves running the syncline,
suddenly inclined downward and out of sight.

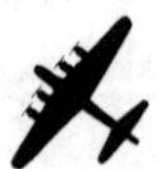

Well, what shall we do for the weekend?
Quiver in a fliver
Shake too late?
By helicopter shoot golden eagles?
Get the rushing feel of running deer to death by snowmobile?
With the motor launch haze grazing whales?

And what shall we do for the deep end?
Assault a park?
Set the final nails in the coffin forest?
Or spray it enough it quickens the unborn
until we ourselves are sick to death?
Assist the dark figure at the outfall?
Await the boatman?
Kill a river?
The Styx is no stranger.
Or we can stay at home in cave light and read Revelations.
Jerk in the dark.

Oh what shall we do for the curtain call
for the rest of our lives end?
And what shall we do for the weekend?

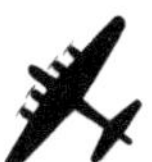

Barbed Wire Boundary

Book 6

Tule Lake Internment Camp

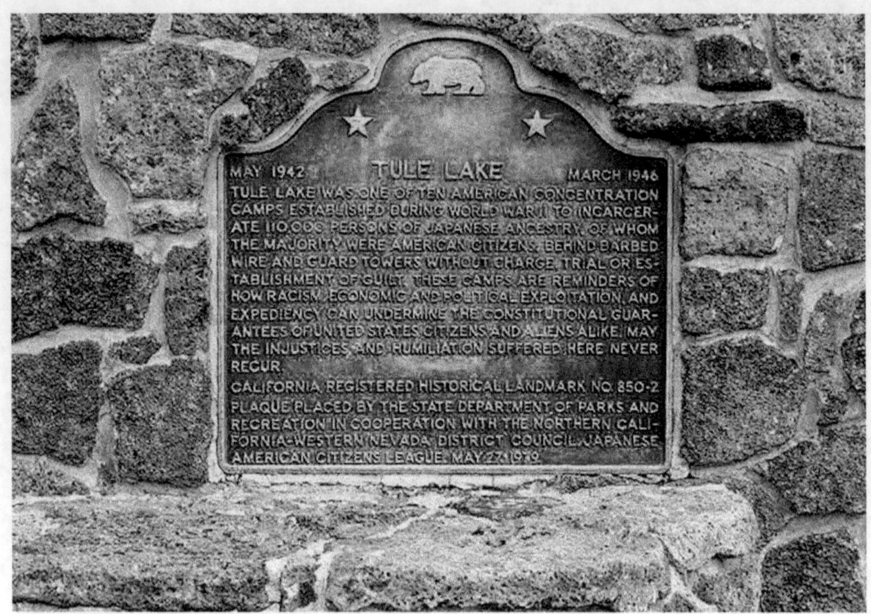

May 1942 TULE LAKE March 1946

Tule Lake was one of ten American concentration camps established during World War II to incarcerate 110,000 persons of Japanese ancestry, of whom the majority were American citizens. Behind barbed wire and guard towers without charge, trial or establishment of guilt, these camps are reminders of how racism, economic and political exploitation and expediency can undermine the constitutional guarantees of United States citizens and aliens alike. May the injustices and humiliation suffered here never recur.

California Registered Historical Landmark No. 850-2.

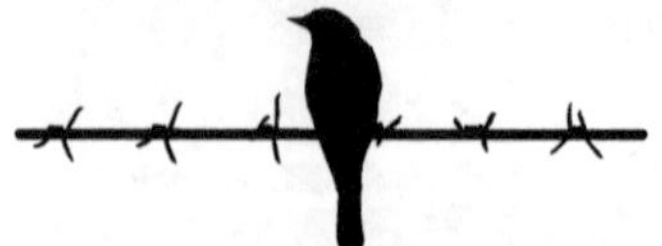

Ode to Japanese Americans

What is this sky without a moon
a sleepless night without its bats?
I have caressed,
no, very carefully examined the darkness
for a sign of life only to find
an arm that I know is very white
and without a single heartbeat.
The black hill beckons, lures me on.
I know there are boundaries.
Somewhere a heart murmurs that it's thirsty.
Somehow the night calls out like a small child,
my name called by unseen children.
So deeply the sun has set
it is unlikely the sun will rise
from such a dark windless night.
I miss the moan of trees
on the black hill.
I stay at home and master hate.
Fingernails in concentration
I found behind the wire at Tule Lake.

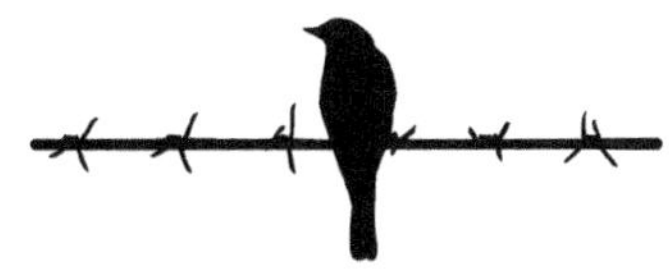

A Poem for Violet

The light is white.
The dream is bright in black wilderness
seized by blue lightning.
An eagle tree many times struck.
The sky changes; is now a book.

There, thunder rolls from within flickering pages
where listed are all the exterminated species.
Now clouds of every feather
This colophon shows its broken wings.

And now the morning wind
mourns across the city,
brings an acid smoke
from our burning obituaries.
Such found wind mixed with phlegm,
gives a splendid account of the future.

Under the tree of wind
with its fleeting load of centuries
I am taking my ease at rest
with the sort of soldier this is.
Eyes are green crystal,
ice, his sober fingers.
Scar-faced, dream-marked.
Together we search the terrain
for the errant blood the sky last had.

Mystery in the colors!
Black basalt with scarlet insinuations.
The stone sentinel is the singing shaman
with his back turned to all humanity.

And, see how the gorgeous, green forest keeps its distance?
For this is gray gravel.
Once that stream celebrated every spring with yellow lilies,
so much blue sky was hung across the glittering flood plain,
with panicles hung out to dry, moving at the margins.
Spring! A stream!
Butterflies drank from the turtle's tears
and omens spread as fingers in silt.
The water, patient in its work, sowing and undermining.

I've come back here
to where they were herded
to find not a single fingernail along the barbed wire fence
left to gouge the naked sky.
The disabled and diseased,
our moral nature undone.

Something in the air,
overhead not a single hawk exists
but brutality and violence
under far stars and dying eyes

And the sky was all violet.
In murderous air.

After the internment in Tule Lake, and shortly thereafter,
one must go back to Hiroshima where Violet returned,
only to find her mother dressed in rags
with hair burnt beyond the roots.

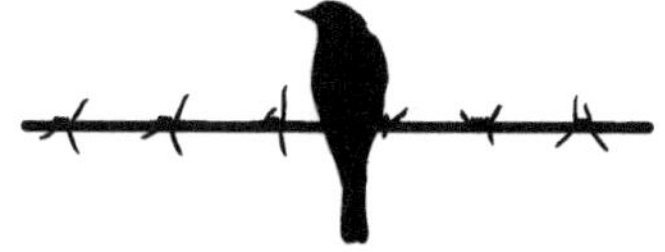

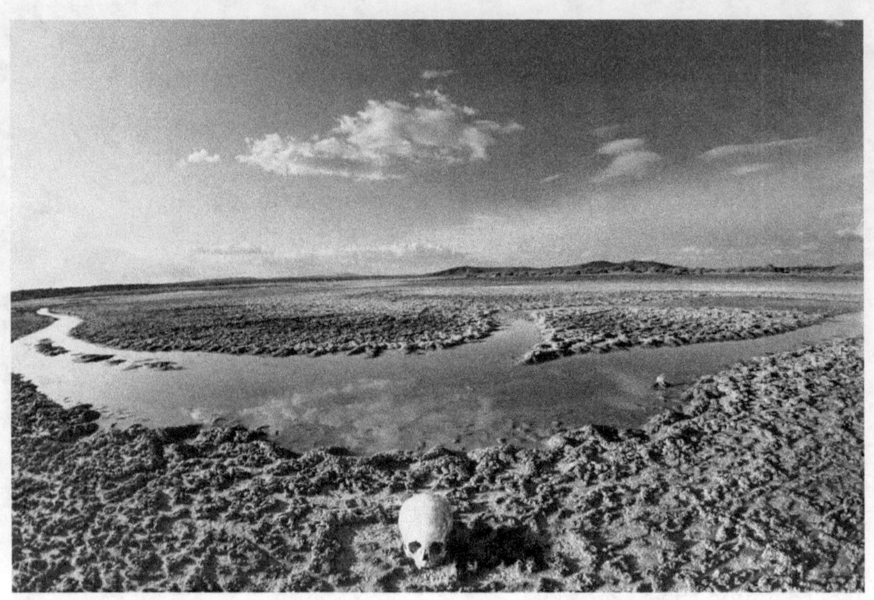

Waving in the wilderness, firs, pines
turned a mule-deer, soft brown under the dense junipers
with my flared scent vanished through curled
leaves in mahogany, mounted then stood and watched me.
Pollen surfaced water, the yellow eddies
curled catkins overhung in black lichen heat
lizards bobbed on their rocks
the resin wind steady on redtail sails,
out in the middle the river splash,
spectacular flash, instant colors the kingfishers beat
I learned to love, lost in summer with sun bleached hair
with cirrus streaks, I laughed with shrieks,
my torn t-shirt, my sunburnt spots,
as I swam out beyond the ripple flows,
floating in pools weasels used.

At Tule Lake not far away
the Nissei children played
where I went as a child to view the
inscrutable nips, but whom, it turned out,
were merely beautiful children
who looked very cold.
In the middle of things was the American flag
standing tall.

They went so easily to those
asylum centers, no asylum in reality,
as the harshest weather hit the barren lands.
I was there—erosion at the headwaters,
the long squirming rivers
incised their gravel beds and banks,
silted the lowlands,
behind the slow precipitations,
the cirques and oxbow lakes drying.

While far away
under guns in towers,
millions stayed, millions prayed
those hopeless useless prayers
useless on the reality.
No one laughed, no one played,
Millions buried, burnt, I heard;
"Millionen unbekannten" it was written,
it was promised "arbeiten macht frei"
lying within the final solution's concentration. *...cont.*

...cont from pg 227

Ages in decline, contagious rages in descending
line and the mountain becomes alert to our ephemeral footfall.
Century in decline, I have honored and photographed
the last eclipse of the century and in my short time
I have witnessed the mountain worn down to fine sand.

We at the margin,
equidistant between the nights, our past,
the days, our future:
Janusian, we see the past
and the future.

The light is still waiting where we loved.
What can we tell these stones?
We have tapped, they have answered,
and now it is our turn.

I think of this when following the old loop of the river
left to the centuries,
when stopped by reality,
this barbed wire boundary.

That charming summer, my child cried,
my child died,
in the green forest silence.

Inscrutable Kingdom Come

Book 7

Endings

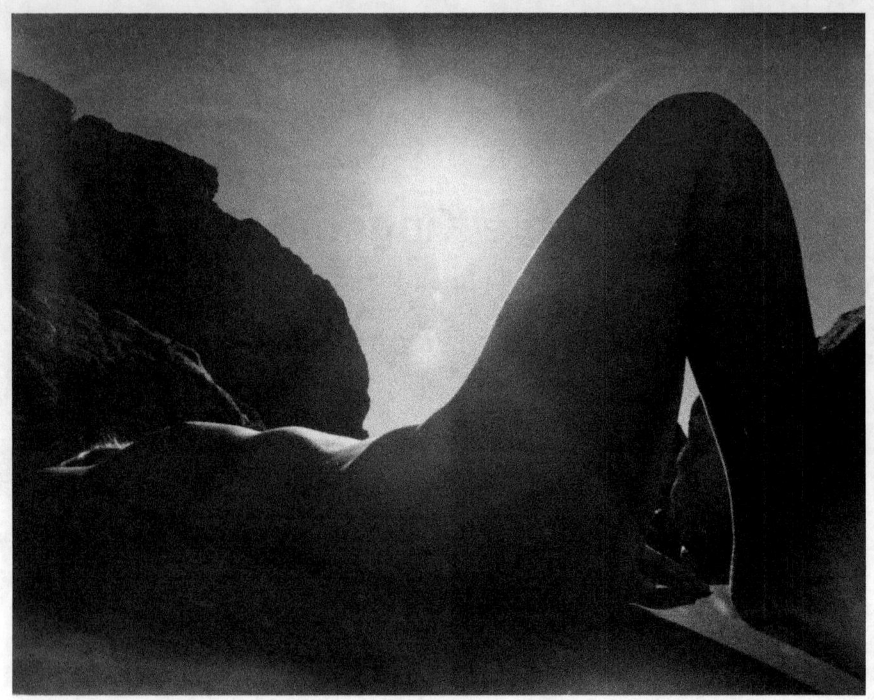

Winter's Onset

Now beached high and dry,
boulders loom whitening with algae
and dying in water's dearth.
Madness has seized the shore
in obsessional memory.

I can show you where they are,
the festive spiders which infect whole boulders
with illusive silk in vertiginous pattern.
Along these stone ramps in plum thickets and chokecherries
is where startled bucks jump twice snorting.

I know of God's footprints in blinding catch lights
and where, near the old shore,
the mariposa hides its bulbs
from an exhausted summer.
I know how the sun sets in fresh deer tracks
along the edge, tracks that fill with water
in the bright silence that reminds me of the eternal,
and our yet temporal presence in a fragile land.

Will you hear me from the other side
where the lake heaves up its ice,
where we lay that nude summer
in full view of the pastured clouds?
Will you hear me
and will you hear the stiff quills crowd the sky
and the tales in the millions fresh from a long journey?

A summer too long dry, revives the deeper roots.
The resourceful light is my love and the hard silence
I carry in my chest is this heavy stone.
It will snow here soon, but the light will not be less;
Straight from the north migratory winds will bring the
gossip of flocks again but I will be less.
I have taken company and conversation with the geese
because I fear to face the winter wind alone.

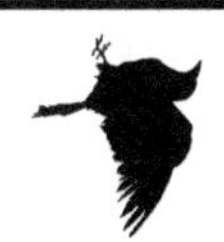

Alone on plains emptied of the living—
desolations, near and far,
but crowded with insistent memories,
milling shadows lose their way in crevices,
within these constancies of stone.

Who among us,
surrounded by every armed guard,
each alarmed by furtive words,
ransomed implacable shades
and nearby piracies,
Who among us will witness the service
as the wind swerves to answer
with cries of our nascence
as rocks mourn the ongoing debacle,
as we in the hill's aisles solemnly follow
the maimed, their exact gestures,
the last rites, as all paths lead to
our senescence?

Who among us?

Strained are trees of this wind,
tethers torn as leaves rain
hours and hours at the sun's arctic angle.
Gone are the herds to their greatest storms
these behemoths, in tangled moss
asleep with eons under
tundra flowers.

And there was so much more than the annual
canticles of snow geese in the millions
echoing in the human ear; woolly mammoths
lying down before their destiny
trumpeting the songs, swans in death remember.

We who are so full of missing.
Who among the best of us
sings such a threnody when
white wings flutter upon grandest dreamers
during their greatest dream?
Sound rushes back as impassioned oratory claiming
ownership to the continent, the virgin forest.

Stone lions roar before the gate, and words,
blue-white flashes, detonate the age
and marl casts up its secret shells, knows its purple veins
in the white clouds squirming in the shock waves.
More is buried with the luscious mollusks yet at work
at their calcareous pinks in green Oligocene.

We were so full of wanting in this life
the length of a dream.

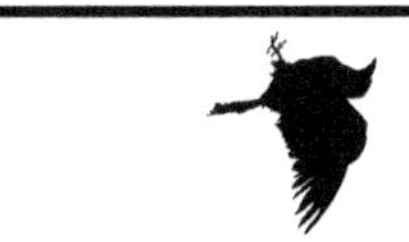

From my chamber
on a shore of shells and empty whispers,
I hear the encroaching ocean, full of voice,
guns pounding, wheeling gulls.
The wild shifting night, heavier than death,
Seethes the waves fast running,
I feel as light as the wandering stone
but hungry as death and fast running.

Why have I built my house from tusks and broken jaws?
My head fills with old men's words, last deeds.
Where did that boaster go,
that crusher of skulls?

Tell me what the river said.
I know that flowers weep
the armada in silence passes
each ship filled with human bones.

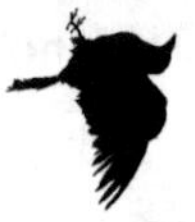

Ground Zero

We are folks waiting in line
in the nervous light of a circus
under spinning lights
A smaller nebula opening for the night
and at the attendant's faltering hand,
our machine also seems played out
on its circuit stopped for all to dismount
for all to board this long night.

Your bright epiphany,
another name for the usual goddess,
forms shining layers at the top of the final stairs,
but it is the end of our entertainment,
our experiment.
It is time we go home.
Now amid the sounds,
now a lull, amid the usual sounds,
these casual owls twitter at
null ground.

Night's long desire and days' rages,
In the moon's last deflation,
under flat bottomed clouds
we were left all alone in this museum,
this grand ossuary.

We expected more than
these cold urns of our ancestry,
this burnt chest of our father's grievances,
charred evidence of our brother's
connivance—grey embers of prodigality.
Fleeting glimpses into
the movement of our history.
Our tickets used up,
we grind down finally
to ground zero.

Dry dust and powdered leaves, the past beckons
the future as an old man wandering aimlessly at the wayside
where the past unattended, unheeded,
explains how our lives threaten the future,
how our not too handsome garment
woven from whole cloth
becomes a winding sheet, our cerecloth.

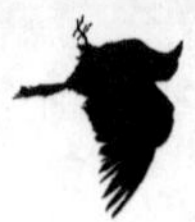

In my evening consciousness,
there's a road I've traveled again and again.
It leads to my father's grave which
I never visited, since its closure.
No tumulus filled with
slaughtered horses and Scythian gold,
just the dead end ends with me.
This sunset I keep in my mind's eye
and watch it like a dutiful guardian,
as if I may never see it again.
But when I wish, it ignites with the sound
of a fuse and with volleys and flares
which salute the shades who
have finally made it to their feet.

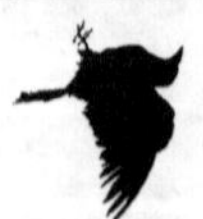

I fall asleep on the day's visions
threading myself through the mind's eye.
Waking in freezing air I stalk,
slipping past winter's deadly gaze.
Rapt, I watch myself; alarmed,
I see my eyes watching:
The hunter's eyes tracking my footprints
through the shrunken crust
of frozen summer leaves stretching
wide like an endless grave.
The fragment moon casts gaunt patterns
on the forest floor phrasing
the same insoluble question:
Why have I turned upon myself?

I've seen my only eternity
leak between my fingers
and now its gone for keeps.

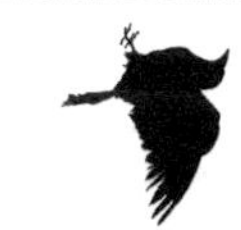

I never knew on my journey
hither and yon,
on a search from pillar to post
never knew what I was
or found where I was
never found the inexplicable why.

Searching yet through graves,
for my mother
and finding only memories of her pathetic frailty.
Under rock finding my father's tokens,
to no avail,
finding nothing more,
only tumult and distress
the depth of the world
this earth's vastness,
the trumpeting of extinct mastodons.

As a grave-born body
grave-torn body
finding, finally my very own bones.

I follow myself at great distance
I have taken time to study the tide and
time takes me.
My birthday goes without saying
and not even my cat knows my name.

With ancestors, *wælsto,* I pace the killing ground
I fear the riptide beyond the estuary
this ruin which again fills with bloated
corpses, each man for himself and
in furious hurry of exile and departure,
the paths where everyone may go
and no one goes home again.

My mouth fills with words I can't comprehend.
When consciousness flows,
my eyes see faces no one likes.
And just like the amnesiac, I can't remember what they told me
like those, the many with dilated pupils that focus at infinity,
deaf to the secrets of their most intricate causeways.
Am I anything more than a long shade in the morning
plundering the earth?

How can I abide this darkness without some mention of the stars?
Black looms with the years and then, as expected, that blazing blue
star rises over the swarthy juniper, joins the foremost among the
first magnitude, completing the symbol and syntax.
How the hours ache.
You must not ask me again what use are my weapons.
You must tell that child with the dove between her palms
that the only thing for her is another poem.

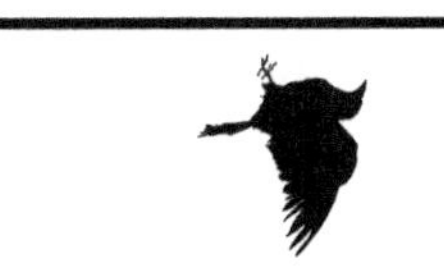

I see the Dog Star and I know of its pup.
I wonder if it's pure aptitude and appetite for
everything that makes us the vilest murderers.
Know that mountain mahogany with its curled lacquered
leaves thrives in dense brakes at the nearly barren flanks.
It's there I shall consign my scarce cold body to the jays
and the pies; after the glut they'll hide the softer parts
under leaves and stones; the bones take care of themselves.

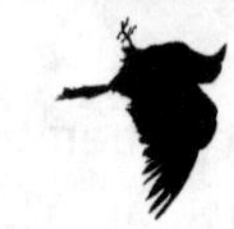

I wait for the finish:
The typist, a real blonde American, an expert
executes my poem, my ready flesh, on a uniform page.
In the splatter, instant electric letters race for the end:
form the scansions', stagger the tabs,
the quick carriage—final bells, ring:
As I wait blindfolded, for the rope: Thirteen knots.
For the gas: hydro cyanide.
For the bullet: twenty eight hundred feet per second.
For the amperage: enough.

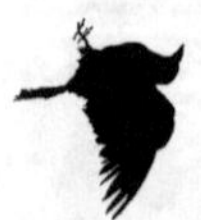

The way takes me away, knowing,
the strident trees stripped, blowing
the limestone eroding, the corroded bronze stands
as a monument by the crater sump,
the fuse finally wrought is twisted stainless steel.
From the layers the rock thrust up,
the student is so astounded to find the earth
turned upside down as it is.

Night and water, black nipples called ripple stones
hoary chinned, I grow younger, dumber in wisdom
waiting, listening for something:
the seepage from dead ferns, new fronds unrolling,
swan calls and other bugling.

From under that palisade of upraised swords cutting
the horizon, I see them now, not barbarians,
not gnarled soldiers made of trees, but the starving, the frightened,
moving forward, billions leaving nothing, not a summer bee,
nor the bee's desert flower. Violent mountains scoured clean and
not even a single locust left in the august jungle.
From the ocean emptiness the ragged kelp lies beached
in legible alphabet.

The Ending

“If this is a game, it’s the ninth inning;
all this is ending,” he said.
“Have you grown tired of human out-croppings,
excrement, ridiculous angles?” I asked.
Some of pseudonym,
many chant acronym: we are sardines and all too aware
of the others packed in, rude and all too close and
with lid peeled back.
I await discovery, headless with the rest.
Is anything as lonely as the melody:
as various and long as the shore line, as lovely
as the French horn?
You confuse the poem with the song I sang
with those clouds whose colors escape you.

Here is the moaning door that gives out on the
blustering shores of gorgeous plovers, but where
light is so cruel all the windows lie broken.

I expect falling glass!
Morning surf is welcome, but flotsam.
Swollen green, this humped ocean glints and groans
in urgent voices and drowns that sadness of the whales’
dirges.

Cease looking for tree lines:
Now landslides of tumbled vertebrae.
The very reason for these long lines I make from
cracked rock and battered crania.

You may view the desert from here, there,
beyond those stunted terminations,
which I have added to the sin-list.
Twilight is rainfall, clear-cut as acid fall
and the antelope's
range is fenced and strip-mined.

Sudden gulls at wind shear cry their maledictions to the lost light.
The patient city trees await the coming of sprawling
forests everywhere, where man and wolf have vanished,
banished without lairs.

Truly wondrous, this blue spruce from ruined
Colorado, but Western Juniper is indicator and
should do very nicely in the new, steady state,
as this earth bears heavily,
on its silent axle.

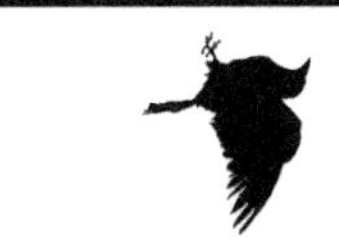

The bittern hides in its own shadow,
the day walks on tiptoe,
fir trees hold their breath,
the lazy line, the shore line
the yellow floating pollen, and I dream.
And the great grey stone is dreaming at the shore,
its steady reflection somewhere here under
the grieving atmosphere. I am alone,
living for a time because that wondrous light
reflected from everything seeks out all
the murkiness.

Days fall back, used up. I've lost my women.
My forest has burned. All my works are now transparent.
Through them I see uncurling fronds
fast clouds full of sleek birds
hounds baying on the trail,
camels in mirage patiently crossing an overheated freeway,
sleeping elephants which were, but could not be.
The cost of hatching eggs, groaning glaciers
a beating rain that might last a thousand years.
The holes in my memory are stars and
the slightest breeze might scatter these words
with my ashes.

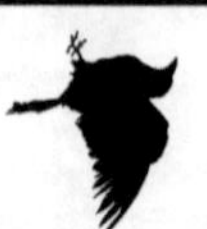

The centuries have caught me and I drag them after me
as I push aside the dreams
and seeing birds, all colors in the evening and there
you were—with the smoke of language.
You spoke with fire and burned with all verbs of being
you called and someone turned inside me: the unknown
persona inside me who stands before the grave in the
garden as the blue horst, its pines in clouds, broods
before the graben.
All colors in the iridescence and the great raven's wing
and the dark heads of evening rear from the pines
and a stark moon assumes its wavering position
between the two yodeling grebes.

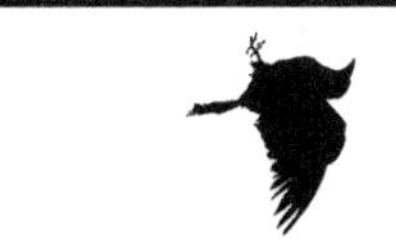

The gash must be abandoned now.
The autoclave won't work,
and the instruments have gone to rust.
Light is failing—life is flickering.
It is the middle of the night
and we have no light left
but candles and the moon.
We have used more hemostats
than the wound could bear
and the bleeding is stronger
than ever, nevertheless.

Whole forests fall.
Our irretrievable tools sink from sight.
Sutures tear and there is no use in closing.
We shall bury the evidence somewhere
in one of those bewildering landfalls anywhere
where the secret is protected by the danger.
Enormous danger protects the secret
for a million years, or more.
One million barrels and the enormity
turns the ocean bloody
and no one knows how
many buried
and the toxic load with which we're stuck.

A forest refutes the debris.
Rootless trees hang upside down,
sliding down with clouds and all the rest that
went up and must come down.

Trees may be rooted with cool asphodels,
when we return,
become a waving forest
if we return.

Did you know we are all
that the sun had hoped for?
Do you know the past is dead,
but still a lesson stays with us,
none the more.
God must yet be born, limping, eyeless,
on the water as the king
if we return, reborn.

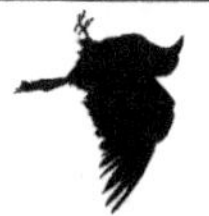

I've studied my position with the forlorn stars.
My position was my inability with the forewarned angle.
Now this the diurnal equinox
ticked down again by these patient hours.
Whose hours were these?
My night time now the same length as my day time.
Daylight roared by with a snort, my too short eternity.
Again I'm caught within fragments of sound,
hurtful as they may be and more.
At the prophetic signal event
the anemic moon has turned blood red.

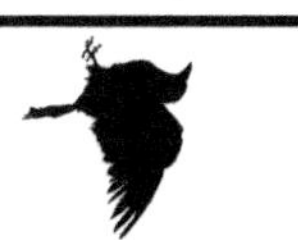

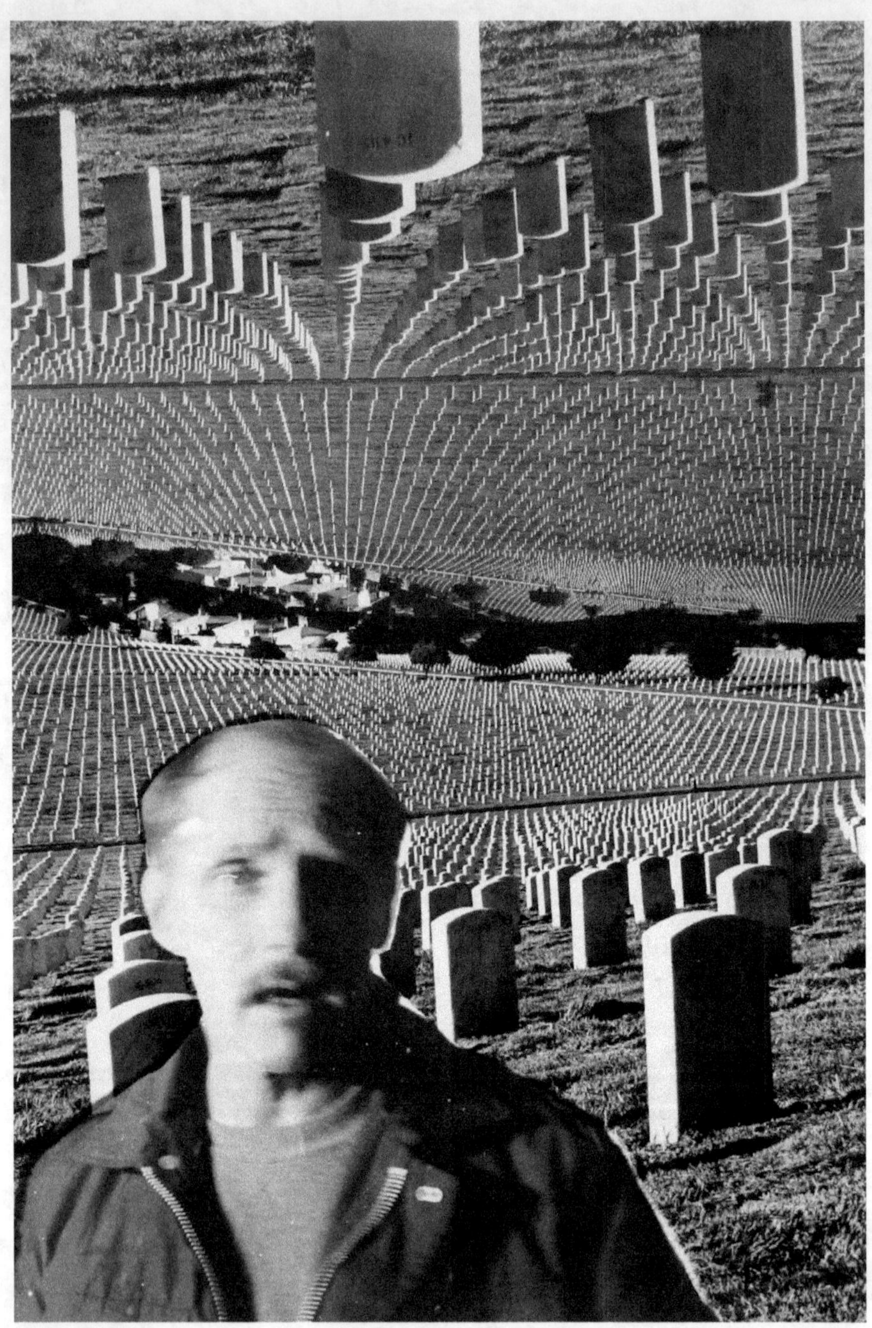

Those who passed here through this tombal land
left only headstones
and because there are no devotees,
the gods have left this exhausted place.

Search as you may no green growth becomes new junipers
because a bird must first eat and pass the seed
before the seed may sprout.
The birds, fewer remaining,
hopeful hospice.

To pursue the ineffable is to find the place,
or should we only place fresh flowers on the stones
to see the flowers wither?

With eyes half closed, listen to the
music the world made before
the shameless ape naked behind his mask
made gods of man and woman.

Before the world is undone,
man must be redone, struggle for the future:
Never for the dead and done for.

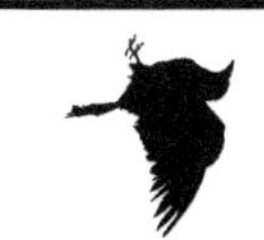

What is she?

Has this woman of all good released all evil?

Oh, did you hear those moaning trees

the forest that kept pace with my life I saw felled

in a single day?

In the long time, the lag time, in the end time

in the memory of theater as death, death as theater,

why must she insist on the ruined silence?

And what is she?

Keep your eyes on the transient actor who will, one day,

in our last defection as the sun bloods up before it dies,

gouge out his own eyes

because he dreams of life he cannot live,

lives for dreams he cannot have.

Some of late search for god the great

in new ordinance

some say sooth

some assign animus to the inanimate.

Now this evening the seven Colossi arise with arms outspread

in slow dance and the clouds they strew have become

the deadly steady state for the new era.

I am leaving now,

I have passed through this century with so many

where so many terrible things have come to pass.

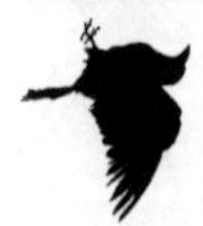

So, my dear, don't console me in farewell clothes:

  good bye, kiss, farewell.

My wrinkles crawl to quiet leather;

  so you know.

Your blue veins stretch to hold your static hands,

  quiet.

Quiet, in cold light my insides shake; your fingers

  cannot find me.

Make my bed a winding sheet

  but I'm unafraid of what you are.

Now, nudge me from my sleep, before I wake,

  before I speak.

In morning movements, green-winged teal race the hour

  in spirals.

Amaryllis grows, the spring shall show:

  cycles are eternal—and I smile.

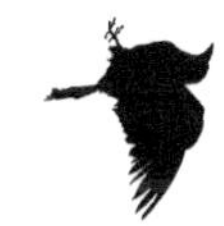

What must have seemed like forever, and was,
no matter what later or future work it was, or will be,
and what's the matter with you, yes you,
who just can't tolerate a little eternity.

Dead at the top this tree overlooks a tide
that carries with it time, iron treads,
and squinted eyes.
My hair has become gray ashes, and I've lost my leaves,
leaves that never again will become leaves,
roots that have lost sustenance,
no matter over what petals or perfume I might tread,
over what land mines I might walk.

Dead at the top, this mountain defends itself.
Never mind the time and the furious winter
filled with crazed and spalling stone
when all of my bright bullets
have become a garden of green tarnish,
and the perfect rifled bore is now the long rusted world
of nuptial spiders.
Twisted as is my own appalling home.
High tide is high time
whelps which whine for their mothers.

Just leave me here.
You don't have to know what I'm doing.
You have no need to know.
Enough to say that my mind mills with ancestors
under arms, astride horses,
on shaking ridges, where dust is torment.

Even though I have dressed myself in stone,
how I miss their loving touches and cruel sneers.
Every pass is lined with braided whips
where all waters have joined the cosmic river,
but I can't say how or why they teach me,
these ancestors who survived in spite of the great Lie.
What would those vengeful mothers have said
of these Kurdish children
trudging through freezing mud, falling forward on frozen fingers,
but they knew a liar when they heard one.
So don't concern yourself with what I drag behind me
on bloody leather.
The fear of death frightens only the living.
Varuna!

Another lie for new liars;
how the moon wanes, how wan.
It is my own panic heart within the child,
my own fear that frights the bird
twittering toward the cemetery.
My sleepless mind is waiting for something.
It's a yellow dog barking all night long.
But God is mute.
Ammon.

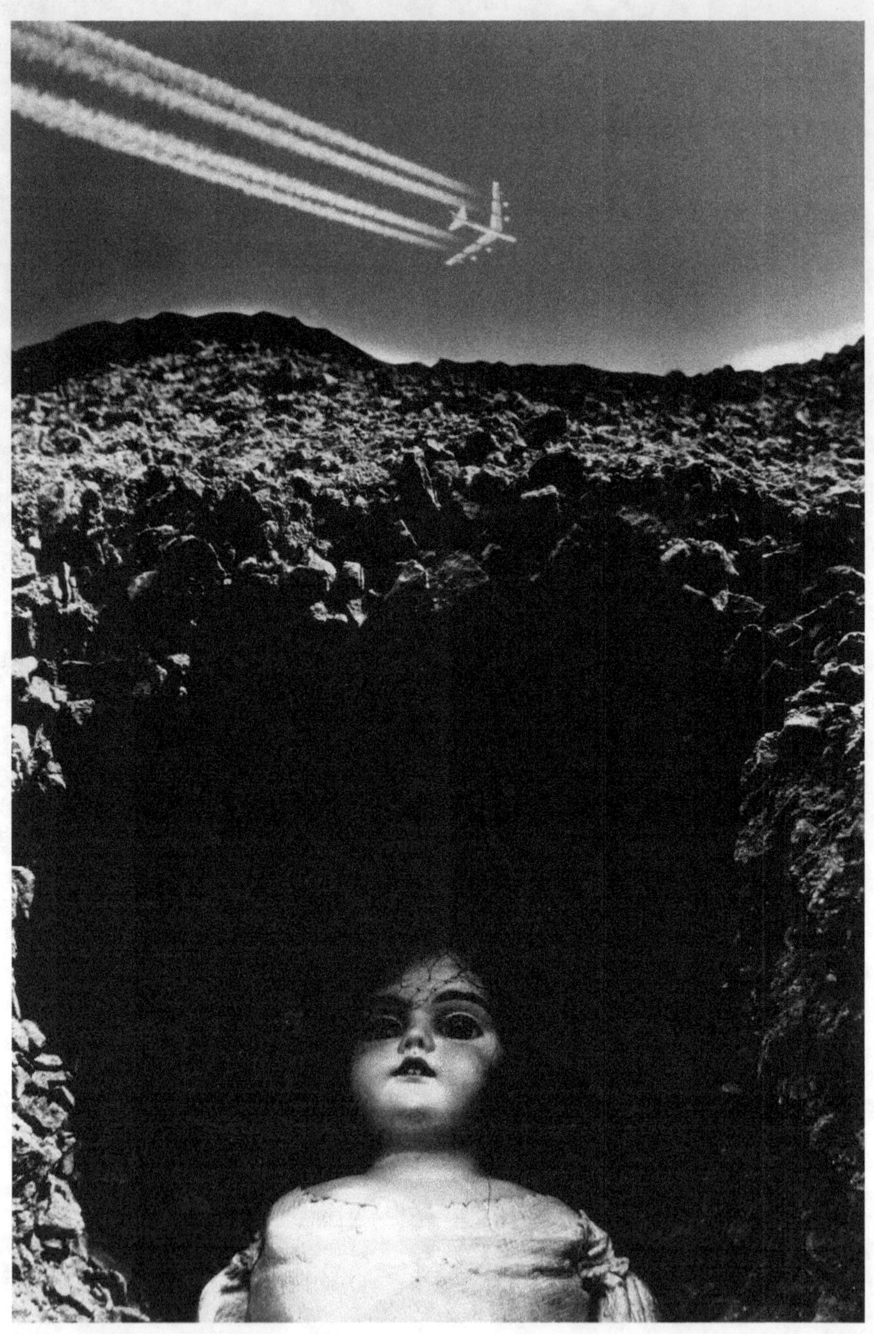

Hard beating shadow, cuts
the mental playa straight, in flight:
night from day, dividing black from white,
sorrow from laughter,
Bird without night, feathered day
of sifting powder,
louder the wind
and the long cirrus eastering
in my mind's eye instant, I fly
free knowing no boundaries
and another magpie flies away
beating fast away from his own shadow.

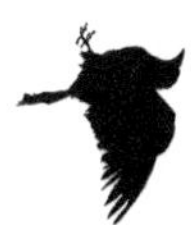

Over head in cloudlessness,
a single contrail ties both horizons together:
friendly skies of United.
One white frost string on a Christmas stratosphere,
higher than blue of indelible Heaven hum,
greater than the Sky God blown from his own
inscrutable kingdom come.

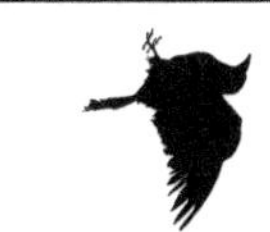

Appendix

Cover Photo - *Earth Rises Over Graves* - WWII veteran graves, Golden Gate National Cemetery in San Bruno. Image of Earth from the moon landing, used with permission, © NASA.

Photo Page 146 - *Den Tiger ist Gleich* - German: The Tiger is equal. Nietzsche. Meaning the Tiger is an equal victim.

Photo Page 156 - *Agent Orange* - 25,513 barrels of 2,4,5-T and 2,4-D,the prime ingredients of Agent Orange crushed by bulldozers in a dump about 60 miles north of Lakeview, Oregon, 1976. Photo published in Audobon Magazine.

Glossary

Page 42 - *stilbestrol (also diethylstilbestrol).* synthetic estrogen used to fatten poultry and livestock, shown by the FDA to cause various cancers in female reproductive organs.

Page 80 - *on mode.* studying the runes in contemplation.

Page 120 - *Ich liebe dich, oh Evykeit.* German: Thus, I love thee, oh eternity. - Nietzsche

Page 161 - *parce que, les jeux sont faits.* French: Because, all bets have been made (a gambling term).

Page 162 - *Per me si va tra la perduta gente.* Dante's Inferno. Italian: Through me you go a pass among lost souls.

Page 200 - *kenning.* In ancient Anglo-Saxen poetry, when the wind is up and it's time to sail, there are white caps on the waves and "the swans are riding."

Page 212 - *yeare iu.* Anglo-Saxen: In the days of yore.

Page 227 - *Millionen unbekannten.* German: millions unknown. Referring to the millions buried at German concentration camps.
arbeiten macht frei - German: work makes you free. From the gates of the former concentration camp at Dachau, Germany.

Page 241 - *wælsto.* Anglo-Saxen: Place of slaughter. Battlefield (of dead Welshman).

Index by Title and First Line

Other works by Lloyd Baker - *Seeing Things,* 1987 (Random House) by Charlotte Painter (Author), Lloyd Baker (Illustrator)

Wasabi Cat Publishing,
Seattle, WA 2015
www.wasabicat.com

www.ingramcontent.com/pod-product-compliance
Lightning Source LLC
LaVergne TN
LVHW020708110826
845149LV00012B/2155

* 9 7 8 0 9 9 6 3 4 3 3 0 5 *